# Nadine and Pamela's Ten Commandments for Changing Careers

**GET ATTITUDE:** No amount of *how-to* can substitute for *I can.*

**LEVERAGE YOUR SKILLS:** Understand what it is that you do well, and use it to your advantage.

**BECOME YOUR OWN VIRTUAL CORPORATION:** Realize that you have the power to become a self-contained business entity capable of marketing yourself to a variety of companies—or starting your own.

**PROMOTE YOURSELF:** Believe in yourself. Learn to brag. Ask for what you want.

**SHOW OFF YOUR SKILLS:** Surpass all expectations. Show *them* what you can do above and beyond what *they* think you're capable of.

**TAP INTO TRENDS:** Follow your passion, but be aware of shifts and trends, no matter what.

**NETWORK:** New technology may be shrinking our universe down to e-mail, but that doesn't mean you can underestimate the power of the human relationship.

**GET A MENTOR:** Thought mentors were just for kids? You're wrong. Get out there and find someone you admire.

**VOLUNTEER:** Not everything you do is meant to last forever. That's why God invented dating before marriage, henna tattoos—and volunteer jobs.

**DON'T LET THE BASTARDS GET YOU DOWN:** Don't forget who you are and what you're made of. Navigate the bastards and their obstacles—there will be many.

# If I Don't Do It Now...

*Career Makeovers for the Working Woman*

PAMELA ROBINSON
*and*
NADINE SCHIFF

POCKET BOOKS
*New York London Toronto Sydney Singapore*

An *Original* Publication of POCKET BOOKS

 POCKET BOOKS, a division of Simon & Schuster, Inc.
1230 Avenue of the Americas, New York, NY 10020

Library of Congress Cataloging-in-Publication Data

Robinson, Pamela.
    If I don't do it now : career makeovers for the working woman / Pamela
Robinson and Nadine Schiff
        p. cm.
    Includes bibliographical references.
    ISBN 0-7434-0783-0
    1. Career changes.   2. Vocational guidance for women.   I. Schiff,
Nadine.   II. Title.

HF5384.R63 2001
650.14'082—dc21

                                                                00-065819

ISBN: 0-7434-0783-0

First Pocket Books trade paperback printing March 2001

10 9 8 7 6 5 4 3 2 1

POCKET and colophon are registered trademarks of
Simon & Schuster, Inc.

Cover design by Tom McKeveny

Printed in the U.S.A.

*To my girls: Hannah, Maddie, Sara, Ruby, and Sarah: May all your dreams come true. And to my son Josh: For being my dream come true. I love you.*

—Nadine

*For my daughter Allison: You fill my heart with love and laughter. I adore you.*

—Pamela

# Contents

*Introduction*
The Working Girls' Blues                                          1

*Chapter One*
Do You Need a Career Makeover?                                   10

*Chapter Two*
The Ten Commandments                                            17

*Chapter Three*
Unzip Yourself: How to Change Your Career                       53

*Chapter Four*
The "Little Black Dress" of Career Makeover Basics             94

*Chapter Five*
Corporate Culture                                              138

*Chapter Six*
If You Can Talk, You Can Sell                                  167

CONTENTS

*Chapter Seven*
### The Internet 178

*Chapter Eight*
### Mind Your Own Business 200

*Chapter Nine*
### Dream Jobs 221

*Chapter Ten*
### If I Don't Do It Now 252

And now a word from our authors . . . 257

Resource Guide 261

Acknowledgments 271

Index 273

# The Working Girls' Blues

We used to think it was hormonal. Standing in front of the open refrigerator, we'd stare at the imaginary Reese's peanut butter cups and perfectly softened Ben and Jerry's. Then we'd wander through the house wondering who had the bad taste in lace curtains and painted furniture. And how about that ceramic pot schlepped back from Italy? Someone had actually bubble-wrapped that hideous object, hoping not to break it on the flight home.

It was a totally dissociative experience. Like Kim Novak in the classic movie *Vertigo,* when Jimmy Stewart makes her dye her hair blonde to look exactly like that other Kim Novak. Only she's not. But he wants to think she is. And pretty soon she does too. And then they all get dizzy.

Our point (yes, there is one) is that every time something went terribly wrong in our lives, we'd be just like Kim Novak: acting like one person, feeling like another. And in our quest for gratification we dyed our hair blonde, gave away the ceramic pot, and ate Oreos. Lots of them.

It took us a while to pinpoint the cause of our despair, but we can tell you that nothing is more therapeutic than watching daytime television in your sweats. Who needs Prozac when you can spend your whole day immersed in melodrama and bad dialogue? When Reva goes back to Josh on *Guiding Light,* and you actually cry at the wedding, you know you're beyond Prozac. You are officially, thankfully, brain-dead.

Ironically, for Nadine, it was her coma state in front of the television that inspired a career-altering epiphany. Lying there, hazily watching all those female journalists, she realized she had the same set of skills as they did, only her wardrobe was sadly lacking. Those women were getting paid to interview people, to put a microphone in the face of someone whose life was in turmoil and who needed help getting out the truth of his or her often sordid story (while boosting the network's ratings). And so, in a manner of speaking, was Nadine. In her role as a therapist she was getting paid to ask emotionally charged questions to vulnerable clients as she attempted to get out the truth of their stories. Except that Nadine, unlike the journalists, had to stick around and pick up the pieces afterward. And she didn't have the power suit or the hundred-dollar haircut.

Nadine knew it was time to pack in her counseling career when she noticed she was spending vast amounts of time counting the floor tiles in her office. That was claustrophobia. Career claustrophobia. And it made her want to spread her wings and do something bigger, for more money, and preferably on location. Realizing she needed to make a big career change, Nadine took what she thought was the next logical step and visited the self-help section of her local bookstore. That's when she learned a valuable lesson. If you read "those" self-help books (you know the ones) when you want to change your career, you really will end up a channel-surfing couch potato. By the time you decipher the hidden meaning of the flow charts and paradigm maps, not to mention the graphs that plot the job market since the Eisenhower administration, your entire life will have passed you by.

Here's what we know. When you're depressed or confused about your job or career, buzz words like *motivation, self-esteem,* and *skill identification* sound like a foreign language. When you're on the brink of despair, frustrated, and anxious to make a change, then self-help advice like "Do what you love and the money will follow" is enough to send you scurrying back to the refrigerator. After all, we love to read on the beach in Bali, but we've never been able to figure out how to make money at it. Besides, our mothers already told us not to believe everything we read.

We *know* you know how this feels. Sometimes, there are so many parts of your life that are out of whack it's difficult to discern just exactly what is bothering you. There are men problems, financial problems, kid problems, and mother-in-law problems—all of which can blend together into one stupefying smoothie.

Fortunately, in Nadine's case, there was a sign. Each time she became anxious about her career she would purchase one article of lime green clothing. If you look in her closet, which you are certainly most welcome to do, you will find a lime green skirt bought when, as a therapist, she knew she could no longer listen to other people's problems. Then there is the psychedelic green sweater purchased when she reached her goal of becoming a CBS Network Television reporter, traveling so much she wasn't quite sure at times what city she had woken up in. And a lime green minidress purchased at a retro shop that the saleswoman said Twiggy had worn on the cover of some fashion magazine. Nadine bought that too, even though she knew she'd never be thin enough to wear it.

Pamela, on the other hand, has kept the same career as a successful executive recruiter for the last thirty years. Always broadening her base to keep ahead of new business trends, always trying to keep up with changing technologies, Pamela began her career out of necessity. She was twenty-one when she found herself in the middle of Manhattan, a single mom without so much as a college degree. Her ambition then was humble. All she wanted, besides the ability to put food on the table for her daughter and herself, was to be able to afford an apartment big enough that she didn't have to talk on the phone while stretched out in the tub.

Pamela began as an assistant to the boss of a PR firm, answering phones and taking messages. But she really wanted to be dealing directly with clients. That's not only because Pamela wasn't exactly born to serve, but because she knew that dealing with clients would allow her to learn more about the business and ultimately help her to move up the ladder. Looking longingly at the women in the corner offices, Pamela noticed that they all wore Gucci shoes and matching Gucci scarves. (This was the seventies, after all.) You can bet she spent a considerable portion of her day thinking about how she could move from where she sat, in borrowed clothes, to one of the corner offices, where everyone wore matching outfits.

Then one day she took it upon herself to write some copy for one of her firm's clients—Vaseline petroleum jelly. Somehow Pamela had figured out, and frankly we don't want to know how, that if you smeared Vaseline all over your legs, not only would your panty hose not wrinkle around your ankles, they would stay up. Who cares, you say? Heloise cared. Heloise was the Martha Stewart of the seventies and the person to whom Pamela submitted her tip. Heloise, being so famous she only had to use one name, thought this was an ingenious idea and printed the tip in her daily column. People took notice, and not only did Pamela show the world that Vaseline was beneficial for more than just chapped lips, she joined the ranks of the Gucci ladies, matching happily ever after.

Today Pamela has her own successful recruiting business with clients such as Disney Channel, News Corp, Sony, Miramax, Danny DeVito's Jersey Films, and Robert De Niro's Tribeca Film Company. And several years ago she accompanied Jeremy Irons to the Academy Awards ceremony. But that's another story.

If you're a working woman between the ages of thirty-five and sixty-five, here's why you may want to read this book. According to the Department of Labor, female baby boomers will have an average of five jobs each by the time they're fifty. We're living twenty years longer than our grandmothers, and ten years longer than our husbands and boyfriends. Since we're living longer, we're working longer. And with our longevity, our dreams for retirement have drastically changed. No longer do we want that condo in Florida with the cute tennis instructor. Too much drama. Now we dream about spending the next half of our lives in another career, doing something we always dreamed about, but never got around to. After a life of climbing the corporate ladder or catering to the needs of husbands, children, and parents, reinventing ourselves has become our passion. Our gift to ourselves.

We're living in an age when the "normal" way of doing things has disappeared, when "What do you want to be when you grow up?" is an outdated question. How about all the things you'd like to accomplish as you metamorphose from girl to woman to sage?

In this career incarnation we want our work to be not only exciting and engaging, but reflective of a lifetime of knowledge gained through our multiple roles as professionals, wives, and mothers. And along with those claims that forty is the new thirty comes an entire generation of women who feel that their role in the workplace is just beginning. Not over. Just the lime green clothing. That's very over.

For us boomers, the more diverse our work experience, the more wrinkles we accumulate, the more marketable we become. The more marketable we become, the less we have to rely on corporations and cranky bosses for spiritual fulfillment and financial security. The gen-Xers have taught us that jobs are no longer life sentences. They are career opportunities, ready for us and created by us as we learn that we can be proactive and make several satisfying career moves in a lifetime. It's not that we don't want that gold watch they used to give after years of service. It's just that we'd rather buy it for ourselves.

We wanted to tell you how to go about changing your career, but in the most accessible, "girlfriend" way possible.

Light on the graphs and charts. Heavy on the humor and empathy. And then we had an epiphany. This one, embarrassingly also inspired by watching television.

While watching a Los Angeles cable show where women undergo makeovers, we were somewhat fascinated as some paramedics of style performed a fashion-emergency rescue. Some nice woman who hadn't bought a new outfit for the last twenty years had been diagnosed with terminal Laura Ashley. She pleaded with the guru, her HMO of fashion, to make her over for her upcoming high school reunion. There were no sirens and no one carried her out on a stretcher, but she did emerge transformed and completely revitalized, sporting a spiffy new haircut and a slimming pantsuit. Even her style doctors pronounced her a miracle of makeover.

*That was it,* we thought. *If you could make over a woman's fashion and makeup, then why not her career?* After all, we spend so much time and effort updating our wardrobes, why not spend time and effort rethinking our professional lives?

To illustrate how to make over your career, we're going to perform three career makeovers on three very different women. We're going to demonstrate that, just like learning how to apply eye shadow in the crease, you can educate yourself to redo your résumé, your attitude, how you use your skills.

Why spend your time reading this book when you could be doing something really important, like improving your wardrobe? That's just the point. We don't think twice about referring to an expert to consult on this year's colors and hemlines. So how about consulting a mentor to aid you in updating and developing new skills for a new career? And

7

just as you would never consider having surgery without talking to informed people that you know, why would you consider making a career change without networking? Remember networking? It's something we did in our *Ms. Magazine* days, then dropped once we got comfortable. And how about updating our knowledge of ourselves and the job market? You wouldn't get on an airplane without this month's *Vogue* or *USA Today*, would you? Why, then, go for years without reading trade journals? Or not taking advantage of the cutting-edge technology?

You know how you used to put a picture of some skinny model up on your refrigerator to motivate you when you were on a diet? Why not take the time to picture for yourself who you'd most like to emulate, someone whose career you would most like to have. Get rid of the fashion model and replace it with a role model. The journey will be much more rewarding. And you'll have to drink much less water.

Why did we decide to write this book? Together, we've logged a lot of years in the workplace. We were there when women first arrived, stayed through the rise and fall of affirmative action and the breaking of the glass ceiling, which, as we always say, we should be so lucky to hit. We truly believe that women, like cats, have nine lives. And we need them to satisfy all of our career interests and dreams. Pamela will give you all the insider information on how to go after another career. Nadine will regale you with her own tales of changing careers three times in three decades. And we'll share with you many stories of how women, just like you, changed their entire career.

If you don't have the time or patience to read the entire book, try this exercise. Imagine you're Susan Hayward in *I Want to Live!* You're going to the electric chair for a crime you didn't commit. You have five minutes to explain to the governor who you are and what you want to do with the rest of your life if you could be granted a last-minute pardon to change your career. Go!

# Chapter One

# Do You Need a Career Makeover?

Maybe you've had something like this happen to you. Rifling through some old magazines, we came across a 1999 issue with Sophia Loren on the cover. It seems this sex siren, who dominated the silver screen with her perfect cheekbones and *don't-mess-with-me attitude* long before the current crop of nymphettes could even pronounce "Marcello Mastroianni," can still make grown men want to catch a one-way flight to Naples. At age sixty-five, Sophia Loren had just been voted "The Most Beautiful Woman in the World." Great . . . but we have to say we have mixed feelings. The good news is that Sophia beat out the young babes like Elizabeth and Julia and Cindy. The bad news is that we know in our hearts that we're never going to look like that. Not now. Not ever. Never going to have cleavage like that. Never going to be able to cook pasta like that. And we are certainly never going to feel so secure that we could marry a man three feet shorter than we are and never blink an eye. Ever.

And so it is with careers. We know you're reading about women in midlife who are becoming CEOs of Fortune 500 companies and "*dot-com*ing" their way into the cyber club and saying "Great," with that same feeling in the pit of your stomach that we had when we saw Sophia Loren on the magazine cover. You're thinking: *It's good that women are advancing and moving up the ranks, but these are other women. I'm never going to have a career like that. Never going to have an opportunity like that. And I'm never going to be able to retrain, reeducate, remarket myself to a fabulous career.* Well, we're here to tell you you're wrong. You absolutely can.

Don't forget girls, who we are and what we're made of. We're the generation of women who fought to pass the Equal Rights Amendment and pushed the Supreme Court to define sexual harassment as employment discrimination, thus making pinching our tushes at the watercooler not only rude, but illegal. We're the women who pressed for the Family and Medical Leave Act and established Emily's List, who wore our hair parted down the middle and subscribed to *Ms. Magazine*. We're the women who founded rape crisis centers and turned *Our Bodies, Ourselves* into the feminist Bible. We're the women who changed things. Hardly surprising, then, that women-owned businesses are employing more and more workers in this country and around the world, or that now, with thirty years of activism behind us, we are in a position to become career activists, proactive women capable of reinventing ourselves and following our dreams.

But wait. What's that you say? Even knowing you're made of the right stuff, you're still feeling burnt out? Always reaching for those Hershey's kisses and trying to hide those little pieces of tinfoil? You're brunette and you want to be blonde? You're blonde and you want to be brunette? You're thinking of renting a house in Tuscany and studying Italian? Or renting an Italian and studying in Tuscany? Here's the real clue. It's time to change your career when you talk to someone who is passionate about what she does, and you're more jealous than when your neighbor bought a sports car convertible but you couldn't because it didn't have a roll bar for the kids.

Staying on the proverbial treadmill may be providing you with security, but chances are those golden handcuffs may also be giving you insomnia and an out-of-control craving for chocolate (or you are like Pamela who had stopped eating altogether). Wouldn't you love to have a career that you could devote yourself to, that turned you on and put fire in your belly instead of the Hershey's kisses? It's not too late.

Stop stressing. All of these feelings are part of our midpoint plateau, our spiritual way station. We're at a point in our lives where reflection and reevaluation are part and parcel of who we are.

For many years we've been on track—the career track, the fast track, the mommy track, or the running track to lose a few pounds—and haven't stopped moving. Well, now it's time. Time to step off the track and take stock of our lives. Time to ask some hard questions. What do we want to do for the rest of our lives? What do we yearn to accomplish? To enjoy? What's our contribution? Our legacy? We don't want to waste what time is left. And what's left is considerable.

All that rabbit food and soy milk have transformed us into bionic women who are living well into our eighties. Those of us in our forties and fifties have a good twenty years of professional life remaining. So if we don't find another career to occupy us, we're going to spend way too much time at Starbucks with the newspaper and cappuccino (triple grande, nonfat) trying to resist buying the cinnamon bun.

**HOT TIP:** Remember, the one-career woman has become as obsolete as the woman who owns only one black jacket.

We're raising the standard for what women in their forties and fifties and sixties are expected to accomplish. Many of us feel much younger now that we're older. Over two million women will turn forty this year. We've had our kids later and our cosmetic surgery sooner, and we are healthier and better educated than ever before. We wear lots of slimming black and don't think twice about taking pills to lower our cholesterol and increase our sex drive. We're getting older but we don't look it. And for those of you who still want to argue that a woman's life is over at fifty, we have only two words for you: *Tina Turner*.

Elaine Kaback, a career counselor and one of our colleagues, often counsels women over thirty-five who are looking to reinvent themselves. "Women come in," she explains, "wanting to get definition in their lives. They're not asking 'What should I do?' They're asking questions like 'What do I stand for?' 'What has meaning for me now?' Now that we've taken off our rose-colored glasses and replaced them with bifocals, we want a sense of worth, of contribution, and productivity."

As Barbara Dixon, one of the women you'll meet in our book, says "When you're a woman in your forties, it's easy to be taken seriously. It's not 'Gee, honey, get me a cup of coffee.' People are more willing to listen to what you are saying. You have experience."

**HOT TIP:** Age is really on our side.

That experience has really built up our Rolodexes, so there are lots of people to call for help. We're not shy. We know time is at a premium. And we know how to pull out all the stops. Denise Jackson, a woman who has had four jobs in the last decade, tells us all to relax. "There is a freedom in being forty. I can say what I want to say. I have enough life experiences. I don't fear failing. I know how far I can push the envelope. The older I get the more I love life."

And the older we get the more we want to savor it. Renée Fraser, a woman who started her own consulting business in her late forties, says moving into another career gets easier as you get older. "Your values change. Your quality of life becomes more important. You don't want to sacrifice everything for a promotion like you did in your twenties. Age gives you the maturity and wisdom to become more persuasive in business. Age gives you credibility. It gives you confidence—without having to flirt."

We are doing well in today's market because we're great communicators and even better collaborators. We know how to mediate and negotiate in a world where young women—and men for that matter—like to win. We are an asset to companies in which young people are often in over their heads in the area of people management. We are loyal. How do you think we survived all those years of sharing bathrooms with our husbands, overtime during the Stanley Cup, and streaks done with silver foil? Loyalty is important. It's also one of the biggest problems in American business today, because the employee retention rate is at an all-time low. It's as if the workforce is holding the career remote and changing the job channel every time it gets bored.

The process of finding another career is not as mysterious as it seems. As you will read in our next chapter, there are ten basic steps to transforming your professional life. Like anything else, you have to start with how you feel about yourself and your attitude about the world and the people in it. After defining what you do best and learning how what you've done in the past can apply to something you want to do in the future, you have to research every aspect of your chosen profession and know everything about it. Then you have to market who you are. If you want to move beyond where you are, you have to show off on the job—always doing more than the job requires, always keeping an eye on future trends. Of course you have to network, find a mentor, and volunteer; but most important, you have to let go of worrying about what other people think of you. Some of your friends and family members may not want you to change. They'll have their own reasons. Everywhere you go there will be men and women who are waiting for you to fail. Don't let them mistake you for someone who gives a damn.

We come from a long line of gutsy women who refused to give up. Through hard work we received the vote, the birth-control pill, and Mrs. Fields Cookies. Florence Nightingale established a nursing school when she was forty, and at age forty-two Rosa Parks refused to walk to the back of bus and started the civil rights movement. Julia Child coauthored

*Mastering the Art of French Cooking* just months before her fiftieth birthday, and may we say, her recipe for coq au vin is divine. Beatrice Wood became a ceramist and potter in her forties and developed a renowned career in the art world. And in her eighties Jessica Tandy won her Oscar for *Driving Miss Daisy*. So what on earth are you waiting for? Study our Ten Commandments for Career Makeovers. As George Eliot said, "It's never too late to be what you might have been."

*Chapter Two*

# The Ten Commandments

For all of our kvetching about wrinkles and sagging, and the memory loss that produces those "senior moments," we know that women over thirty-five rule. We may have exercised terrible judgment in wearing tie-dye shirts and had the audacity not to trust anyone over thirty, but now we're changing our tune. Big time. That's because we're over thirty ourselves and do not want to be excluded. No one could accuse us of being stupid.

Why is it so hard to make a career change? The irony is that for many of us the sexual revolution and the power suit didn't do a lot for our self-esteem. In fact, a lot of us still deal with the same issues we encountered all those years ago: unequal pay for work of equal value, the boys' club, and sexual harassment. Women still must decide how to balance the demands of their career with family needs. Given that we were in the workforce when the glass ceiling was considered an avant-garde architectural innovation, we have lots of practical advice on how to change your career.

Thirty-two years ago, Pamela was hired by the Taft Personnel Agency at Forty-fourth Street and Madison Avenue in New York City. Her boss, an executive of the company, told her to change her name because, and we quote, "It's too Jewish, and most of the companies you'll be working with are anti-Semitic." Desperately needing that job in order to support her infant daughter, Pamela allowed him to change her name from Pamela Katz to Pamela King—and thus became the first woman the Taft Personnel Agency had ever hired. That's how she earned the right to talk about issues like the good-old-boy club, affirmative action, workplace discrimination, mentoring, and being the only woman in a company of fifty people.

Pamela's first business call on behalf of Taft was with the vice president of human resources at the Celanese Corporation. The man, about forty years old, was an ex-Marine Corps sergeant and the epitome of the buttoned-down executive: crew cut, white shirt, wing tip shoes, rep tie, and black framed glasses. Pamela can still picture him today.

The fear of failure was always Pamela's strongest motivator, in addition to her overwhelming need to make money. Twenty-one years old, a single mother with a two-and-a-half-year-old daughter to support, she had no other choice. She had to succeed. Looking at this man—and he *was* intimidating—Pamela was fearful. But she managed to maintain her composure as she shook his hand and sat down opposite his desk. "What makes a young woman like you think you can place CPAs and financial executives with Celanese?" he barked. "You have no financial background, and besides, how old are you?" She knew she had to think quickly and be smart—or else she'd be out the door. Failure was not an option. So, drawing on reserves from who knows where, Pamela told her potential client that, while she was not a practicing CPA, she did know the parameters for accounting jobs. Besides, she continued, it was not necessary for her to have a financial background because the important function of a recruiter was to interview well and be able to assess and judge all of the intangible characteristics of a candidate—not just those that are apparent from a résumé. Yes, she said, she was young, but she still had the innate ability to evaluate a candidate's work ethic and business philosophy. Moreover, she was an excellent judge of character and could evaluate the various personality traits necessary to perform the job well. Pamela thinks she remembers breathing a silent sigh of relief as she heard the words come out of her mouth. She's not sure. What she does remember is the look on the executive's face—he obviously was impressed, as he became her first client.

As for Nadine, when she cohosted a television talk show with three guys back in 1980, it was assumed she would do the fluff pieces. Hard to believe, but at that point a lot of people doubted that women were capable of handling hard news. Big mistake. The cooking shows were bad enough, but one night while introducing a magic act, the dry ice machine went awry, leaving Nadine ankle deep in water and holding a live microphone. Not only did she almost succeed in electrocuting herself, she almost blew up the entire studio because she didn't step out of the water fast enough. After that incident management thought it would be less risky for Nadine to simply do interviews and read copy. Which is how she found herself out of the fluff news business.

So as you climb your professional mountain, here are the Ten Commandments for changing careers, written by a couple of broads who've been around the block and climbed a couple of mountains themselves. Unlike the original Ten Commandments, these aren't written in stone . . . which makes them a lot easier to read on an airplane. So skip the forty days and nights in the desert and start your own career makeover here.

## The First Commandment: Get Attitude

*No amount of* how to *can substitute for* I can.

We cannot emphasize this enough. You must cultivate self-confidence and a willingness to get out of the good-girl role of being seen and not heard. You must. Being able to see yourself in a positive light and market yourself strongly and proudly is essential if you want to open yourself to any kind of change.

Our image of ourselves determines how high we go. If we're able and motivated, but can't envision ourselves in a prominent position, then we'll sabotage ourselves. Coming into a job interview with enthusiasm and confidence creates a great impression. You're not the only one who feels that life is too short. Employers feel that way too. And here's a little secret: No matter how much they doth protest, they're going to hire the candidate they like the most, not the one with the best qualifications. Even if the company has to train her a little more.

Not only does your attitude determine your likability factor, it can also make a crucial lasting impression. Debbie Myers tells us the story of being young and inexperienced and being given a free pass to a movie screening. The theater was crowded when she arrived, but she could see empty seats beyond the velvet ropes, so she lifted up a rope and sat down in the plush area reserved for guests and dignitaries. The publicist, an intimidating kind of guy, came over to her and politely asked her to leave. This area was reserved for special people, he explained. Debbie shot back that this, then, was the perfect seat because she was indeed special. She went back and forth with the guy, tenaciously holding her ground until he let her stay.

Fast-forward several months. Debbie was now applying for a publicity job at one of the Hollywood studios, and there were hundreds of applicants. She went into the interview, and, lo and behold, the interviewer was the intimidating guy at the velvet rope. (Yes, we know this sounds like a cheesy Hollywood movie—where do you think they get their ideas?) Not only did he recognize her, he did an amazing thing. He hired her on the spot. Because, he said, if she's capable of holding her ground with him, she'll certainly make a great publicist. Debbie's confident attitude paid off. Big time.

Attitude is all about confidence and self-esteem. Knowing who you are, accepting who you are, and above all, valuing who you are. Remember what your mother told you before that first date? *Be yourself and have fun.* Great advice. And

21

it holds true for interviews too. Going out for an interview is a little like going out on a date. Both parties know whether they are having a good time or not. If you don't feel good about yourself, an interviewer will pick that up in a nanosecond. If you are nervous and have cold hands and a sweaty handshake . . . that's a red flag for an interviewer. If you react that way for an interview, how will you handle the pressure of a presentation? If you are shy or feeling vulnerable and don't allow your inner strength to shine through, an experienced interviewer will question your ability to perform under pressure and to work in a high energy, fast-paced environment. So be sure you're in a positive frame of mind, and look that executive straight in the eye, smile, and extend your hand for a firm, confident handshake.

Lynda Lytle, an entrepreneurial business consultant, insists it's easier to change your career in your forties because that's when we have the most self-confidence and experience. She says, "Now I know my capabilities, and I have great client references. I'm focused on my business and have confidence in my choices. As a woman in her forties, I have experience and maturity. Look at all the high-tech companies now. Xerox and Hewlett-Packard have women as their company presidents. Being female and over forty is now a definite asset. I carry that knowledge with me, and it shows."

HOT TIP: Verbally rehearse your strengths so they are on the tip of your tongue and you don't have to stop to think what they are when someone asks.

It's important to do things that give you confidence. Anything. For Susan Frank, former executive vice president of

Odyssey Entertainment, playing team sports gave her the confidence to play competitively at work. Volunteer work, creative endeavors, and sales (a great confidence builder) can also help. But most important of all is to be in relationships that validate you. There's no point in building yourself up only to have the people around you tearing you down. If you're in that self-destructive cycle, sadly, nothing in this book will help. You've got to take stock of yourself, allow friends to give you some helpful feedback, and perhaps get some professional counseling. You've got to know what's holding you back before you're ready to move on.

We conclude our First Commandment with a great piece of advice for women over thirty-five. Age is all attitude. As Cynthia Cleveland, president of Universal Studios Consumer Products Group, says, "Just like when you take the leap of faith to get married, or commit yourself to an enduring relationship, so, too, must you take a leap of faith when you change careers. There is no perfect time to make that move. Just do something and adjust. Overcome your fear, because short of death, there's nothing that a good attitude can't alter."

## THE SECOND COMMANDMENT: *LEVERAGE YOUR SKILLS*

*Understand what it is that you do well, and use it to your advantage.*

There is a practical way to go about making over your professional life, and you don't necessarily have to mainline antianxiety medication to get there. Changing careers doesn't have to mean burning your bridges, turning your life into an apocalyptic mess by running off with your yoga teacher, or going back to school to incur a deep debt. Better to take the skills you already have—the talents you've already accumulated—and transfer your marketable experience into another area. Understand specifically what it is that you do well, use those skills to your professional advantage, then go for whatever career you desire.

Determining your skills is a difficult and time-consuming task—but a must. Consider these four main categories of skill sets. Be aware that you probably possess a combination of two or more skill sets. Where do you fit in?

**Analytical Skills.** You are "left-brained." Your tote bag is completely organized. You are analytical in your approach to problems and not a shoot-from-the-hip kind of woman. Forget your astrological chart. You know who you are. You're a strategic planner or maybe a systems or financial analyst. You just glance at the grocery bill and know if you've been scammed. Mathematical by nature, you are the one who adds up the check and tells everyone what they owe, plus a tip. The rest of us respect and despise you.

**People Skills.** You motivate people. Your staff loves you. You are always bringing together different personality and skill types to collaborate on in-house projects. You even get them all to buy Girl Scout cookies (chocolate mint, of course) from your favorite niece. Your local SWAT team may not know to call on you in a hostage situation, but everyone in your company knows you have great negotiating skills. You give great talk and are a fabulous presenter. You're one of those "luckiest people in the world" that Barbra Streisand sang about.

**Creative Skills.** You are "right-brained," a conceptual thinker. You are a graphic artist, a print designer, or a writer—maybe a high-paid creative executive in an industry such as entertainment or advertising. You are also a visionary, a person who is able to translate ideas into pictures, words, or sounds. You have the inherent ability to see the world differently from most others. You are constantly losing your keys and eyeglasses, but people forgive you. They know you have more important things to ponder.

**Manual Dexterity.** You may be an artist, painting or sculpting to express yourself. Perhaps you knit or sew and are thinking of taking what you learned in your high school economics class and turning it into a profitable cottage business. You are great with your hands. You can use power tools and can apply mascara in a moving vehicle. You're the one who fixes the dripping faucet and opens the jam jar, the one to slide the coat hanger into the window of your car when you've locked yourself out. Other people have your number on speed-dial.

It is crucial to be able to define your skill set and to articulate your skills in precise language. We've started you off with a broad base; what you have to do now is list your own skills. Here's how to go about it:

- Recall your accomplishments. Consider all aspects of your life, not just your working life. What about passions, hobbies, and community work? There are skills involved in doing the most mundane activity. Everything you do counts. Don't forget your secret ability to make a soufflé that never collapses in the oven. That reveals admirable precision. Don't forget your personal skills as CEO of your own family. Ten to one you are a budgeter, a juggler of multiple tasks, and a homework professor capable of closing a deal over the phone while assembling a lasagna. Think of the skills in doing all that.

- Now narrow your thinking down to your current job. List all the things you do on a daily basis, and break down the functions inherent in each activity. Include all the small tasks, such as running meetings, administrative duties, and scheduling—even figuring out how to refill your stapler.

- Ask your boss or your human-resources representative for a current job description. This will serve as a catalyst to help you decide which skills to list on your résumé, some of which you may have forgotten or may never have thought of before. Now work backward, analyzing your prior positions. See what skills you've acquired in past jobs, and apply them to what you think you want to do now.

- Tally your awards, speaking engagements, continuing education courses, and trophies. What skills do they acknowledge?

We're willing to bet that this exercise took longer than you thought. You didn't realize you had so many talents, did you? Great. But this is no time to rest on your laurels. Now that you've defined your skills you're going to have to learn how to articulate them. You're going to have to learn how to show the world that your skills will transfer from one career to another. Consider this.

Cynthia Cleveland was successful in the toy business, but wanted to move into a new industry. Teleflora was hot at the time, so when an opening there came up, Cynthia wanted to know how on earth she could transfer the skills she had learned in the toy business to the flower business. With a little bit of research and a lot of ingenuity, she was able to articulate to Teleflora concisely and specifically the similarities between the two businesses, showing how her skills could transfer from one to the other.

Cynthia explained to the folks at Teleflora that flowers, like toys, are a trend business. They're both about fashion, color, and style. Both are seasonal businesses that are holiday oriented, and both require a production lead time of about a year and a half. She was accustomed to thinking seven months ahead in terms of what the consumer would require, and she made sure that Teleflora knew she understood the value of forward thinking and planning ahead. Cynthia also wisely pointed out that overall strategic marketing concepts are universal, and that she could apply what she had learned at Mattel to the flower business. Both businesses required creative and management skills, and again, Cynthia made it clear that these were skills she possessed in abundance.

Teleflora was very impressed with her parallel skills, and her articulation of them. But had Cynthia not defined her skills, she wouldn't have been able to transfer them from one career to another. And Teleflora would still think of her as that bright woman who worked in toys and too bad they couldn't use her in flowers.

The ability to bring the tricks of the trade from one industry to another is always appealing to potential employers. And although we may offend some people by saying this, often the interviewer isn't very imaginative, so being specific about your skills, using illustrations and examples to demonstrate how your skills will transfer is necessary. That's why you have to expand the definition of yourself—as someone with a set of skills that can be applied to almost anything you want to do.

By assessing your skills and determining your strengths, you can begin to leverage yourself into a new career or into another job within the same career. We know you. You are an absolutely fabulous composite of all kinds of great qualities and gifts. What matters is how you apply those gifts to your chosen venture.

## THE THIRD COMMANDMENT: *BECOME YOUR OWN VIRTUAL CORPORATION*

*Realize that you have the power to become a self-contained business entity capable of marketing yourself to a variety of companies—or of starting your own.*

If you hear the music from the *Twilight Zone* as soon as you see the words *virtual corporation,* don't stress. We are not diverting you to cyberspace, nor are we trotting out a fancy term just to see if you understand it. A woman who is a virtual corporation is the professional equivalent of "chief cook and bottle washer." Or the symbolic woman in a power suit with a briefcase in one hand and a baby in the other. Relax. We're not suggesting you buy into the eighties myth of the superwoman, so put away those shoulder pads. We're advising you to recognize the extent of your reach, to understand just how much you can do, and to use it to your own advantage by thinking of yourself as a virtual corporation.

As a virtual corporation, you are a self-contained business entity capable of understanding and operating any facet of your profession or industry. You have the skills to market yourself to a variety of companies or to start a new one. You are continually learning and improving yourself, keeping up with trends within your field and others. You take courses to keep yourself updated, read trade journals and business magazines to keep you in the know. You network, attend conferences and trade shows. You are a research machine, and the people who know you all want to sit next to you at dinner because you are as current as the front page of tomorrow's newspaper.

Lynda Lytle says that packaging yourself is everything. "People make up their minds about you very quickly. That's why you have to present yourself as a virtual corporation. I am actually a corporation of seventy people scattered across the United States. That's because I have an extended Rolodex of every person I've worked with on every project." The important thing is to recognize that we have years of history, which means not only experience, but contacts. Our past can be found in our Rolodex. For women starting their own businesses, using this network of people as potential clients or as a bridge to future clients is imperative. When changing jobs, network with everyone you know. You never know which contact will pay off.

The way to be an autonomous entity is to be a Ms. Know-It-All . . . and that requires research. Research is the significant factor in staying a virtual corporation. Today's marketplace is fast and competitive. You need to constantly be aware of all the changes in technology, all the mergers and acquisitions, as well as executive movements within your industry. If you're interviewing with a new company, it's important to understand its position within the marketplace. If it's a publicly held corporation, then be sure to read the annual report. Not only will the annual report give you the financial details, it will also give you a description of all the divisions within the company. This is extraordinarily helpful because your notions about a major corporation are naturally formed by its known products and brand names, but that's not the whole enchilada.

Always be the exemplary dot-com girl and check out the company's web site. Remember, all the other candidates are walking into interviews armed with the latest news on the company gleaned from the tons of business news sites that are so easily "clickable." The company web sites will give you the biographies of some of the key people. Find out what you can about them, and don't forget to familiarize yourself with the company's product line too. And by the way, there is a kind of code among interviewers. If you bring up something in the interview that can only be found on the web site, that is the signal to the interviewer that you have gone the extra mile and done your homework. It's the professional equivalent of Carol Burnett tweaking her nose at the end of her show, or the catcher holding out three fingers to the pitcher.

**HOT TIP:** Know the competition of the company you want to work for and how they operate. Talk to people in competing companies and see what you can learn.

Check with your investment adviser for Wall Street's opinion of the company in which you are interested. And what about the forecast for the industry as a whole? Your investment adviser (and it could be your college roommate's brother-in-law) will have access to a wealth of current information, so take advantage of this additional input. Go on-line again and check out a variety of analysts' recommendations, as well as the history of the stock. You may want a challenge and would be excited to join a company in a turnaround situation. You may want to work for a company in trouble so that you can have the opportunity to use your skills to breathe life and profitability into the organization. Or you may want to work for a solid company that has a slow but steady growth pattern. By accessing your broker's or financial adviser's information bank, you can find out all of this pertinent info, both on-line and off. Most women don't think of this, but we weren't born yesterday . . . even if sometimes we wish we were.

You should also go on-line to see what other jobs are offered in your field on job sites like Monster.com or jobs.com. Nadine found a site called Job Sleuth, which came up with six openings for journalist jobs across the country. There was also one listing for a star quarterback, but, sadly, she lacked any transferable skills.

In the end it's important to do research on the company you're interviewing for. If you know who they are and you know who you are, then you can convince them you're a perfect fit.

# THE FOURTH COMMANDMENT: *PROMOTE YOURSELF*

*Believe in yourself. Learn to brag. Ask for what you want.*

Now that you have become your own virtual corporation, you have to get the word out about how incredible you are. You have to market and advertise yourself. One of the problems many women face is their inner reluctance to take the stage, front and center. As Renée Fraser, a PhD psychologist with her own consulting firm, wisely points out, "We have to learn to showcase our abilities and take credit for our work." That means keeping our profile high and not sitting in the corner like some wallflower at a Sadie Hawkins dance. We have to get out there and take the lead.

In case you're one of those dinosaur women who steadfastly refuses to wear white after Labor Day, you may have missed the fact that it's totally in vogue to brag about your work. Get your Master of Hype and develop an I-am-so-talented-I-blow-myself-away mentality. It's necessary if you want to survive this spin-cycle world.

Susan Gordon, currently West Coast director of the American Friends of the Israel Museum, says self-promotion is imperative. "I got passed over for a promotion. I was a good girl and didn't know how to toot my own horn. After all, we were not supposed to be too competitive or too aggressive. I had a fear of sticking my neck out. I know now you have to be prepared to show your boss why you should get that raise or promotion. After all, your boss is not a mind reader. Let your desires be known. Toot your own horn."

Not many women are brilliant self-promoters, but the first step in creating a new career is to reinvent yourself. No matter how many careers we have in a lifetime (and according to the Department of Labor, we're likely, on average, to have five), we must create a "brand" or reputation for ourselves. We must put ourselves forward so that we will be respected and trusted for what we stand for. Rid yourself of the notion that only men display such bravado. To change careers, you must be able to sell yourself. Sadly, many of us would rather submit to torture than be in the position of "talking up" our achievements.

**HOT TIP:** Resist the temptation to say, "I was lucky." Take credit for your accomplishments.

Believe you are great, and have the confidence to say who you are and what you've done. If you feel good about yourself, you'll feel comfortable about being visible and will take risks to alter your career course.

Renée Fraser's advice? "Merchandise the hell out of yourself." Don't be afraid to take the spotlight. Make speeches. Become driven. Use every interview you have, whether it be informational or in response to a job advertisement, to promote yourself. The best way to lift your experience off the page is to articulate how savvy and adept you are in an entertaining fashion. Don't be afraid to show them that you're fun. We're not suggesting you make your entrance on a Harley, but let them know you have a sense of humor and that you'll be easy to take around the office.

Here's another hot tip from us to you. When they ("they" being the corporate muckety-mucks) ask if you can do something, just say YES! Never say no. Don't admit you don't know. That's the difference between twenty and forty. Or fifty and sixty. You're resourceful. You're smart. You'll figure it out.

## THE FIFTH COMMANDMENT: *SHOW OFF YOUR SKILLS*

*Surpass all expectations. Show them what you can do above and beyond what they think you're capable of.*

Show off your skills in a professional setting. Go beyond your job description and do more than what's expected of you. Way more. Leverage your present job by moving around within your current company. Identify problem areas and volunteer to work on them. Ask your boss what he or she sees as the obstacle to proceeding to the next important project in the pipeline. Offer to help. Make it known that you are eager to expand your responsibilities. Your long-term success depends on the value of the projects you work on, so why not take an unassigned task and run with it. There's no better way to stand out.

Lynda Lytle, now an entrepreneur with her own consulting company that services major clients such as Levi Strauss and

General Electric, tells us that during her twenty odd years in management, she made several lateral moves within Xerox because she wanted to learn as many job functions as possible. After five years of seeing what drove the company and what created momentum, she moved freely in and out of every department. "Within Xerox Learning Systems, I planned all the seminars to train the trainers to sell Xerox products," she says. "I volunteered to go out with the sales reps to help them close the deals. I realized there was more money in sales than in training, where I was working, so I made my relationships and was able to segue into the sales area. I learned about the company's hot line and customer service department, and that helped me make the next strategic move into marketing. Part of showing off is strategizing and planning ahead."

The best and easiest way to forge a new career path is to identify certain problems in your company or within another organization, then come up with a strategic plan to solve the problem. That kind of initiative will brand you as innovative and cutting edge. Every time. And in the process you will market yourself as a person who's self-driven. A definite plus.

Pay attention to what's happening within your company, especially if it's outside your office and your immediate job function. If you hear that a task force is forming to analyze new trends, track down the leader and offer to be part of the team. If you see a newspaper or magazine article pertinent to your business, send copies to your boss and peers with your comments. Organize regular lunch seminars to exchange thoughts and ideas. Participate in industry organizations. Give public speeches. Make yourself visible. Let your boss know how you're doing. Don't be afraid to show off.

Imagine yourself as a stand-in waiting in the wings. One night, the diva gets the flu and "they" are desperate for someone to replace her. And you are there, skills ready and waiting, with documented proof of your competence. Because of your extra work beyond the call of duty, you are seen as a major player. Ready for the spotlight. And your close-up. Not to mention your promotion.

## THE SIXTH COMMANDMENT: TAP INTO TRENDS

*Follow your passion, but be aware of shifts and trends. No matter what.*

When we think of how important it is to stay ahead of business trends and technology, we always imagine the woman at the conference table who, twenty years ago, forecasted life on other planets. We imagine her urging her coworkers to extend their business visions to include satellite communications, since we would soon be a wireless generation. We bet her bosses couldn't bring on the butterfly nets fast enough. It's harder to deter creative thinkers these days, mainly because the dudes in garages have become millionaires. But if we've learned anything from the new millennium and the new technology, it's that we must stay current. The last thing any of us wants is to go back to the typing pool. So, make sure you've learned the most important lesson of the Internet generation (no, not how to order your accessories and cosmetics on-line): get connected and stay connected!

Currently, computer technology is one of the major influences in society, including of course, the Internet. Look into the new-technology associations that have sprouted up over the last three years. Check out the new-technology magazines such as *The Industry Standard* and *Silicon Alley Reporter* to find out who's who and what's what. In Los Angeles, the Venice Interactive Community (VIC) was one of the first tech networking organizations to form. What started as a local, homegrown meeting place has burgeoned into a major networking organization in the Internet field and a formidable force in the high-tech industry. These groups attract aggressive, hip, and fast-track up-and-comers—people from whom you can learn a lot of information. Attending and networking this way keeps you in the know.

Important trends can be identified in just about any area of work, as Barbara Dixon well knows. In 1974, Barbara went to work on the legislative staff of Senator Birch Bayh, a Democrat from Indiana. As the only woman on the staff of forty and low person on the totem pole, she had a hard time being taken seriously by the senator's legislative director, who dismissively assigned her "women's issues." One of the issues affecting women which immediately captured Barbara's attention resulted from a Supreme Court ruling disallowing pregnant workers protection against employment discrimination, in particular the right to receive disability insurance. The court's ruling in the Gilbert decision galvanized national women's organizations which were outraged at the court's action. Meetings to draft legislation to overturn this decision resulted in coverage by all national broadcast networks—much to the stunned surprise of the senator's legislative director.

Barbara was able to mobilize a nationwide lobbying effort for the legislation she and her able senator drafted, resulting in the passage of landmark new protections for pregnant working women. The argument to overturn the Supreme Court was so compelling that the legislation only received four votes against it. As a result of the legislation that she initiated and subsequently helped to pass, Barbara got a mailing list going that turned into a major bankroll for future campaigns. And an insider's role on the senator's staff.

Barbara recalls that she caught a terrible cold from working so hard. Boxes of tissues lay next to her on the Senate floor, and afterwards, she slept for a week. But it was all well worth it in the end.

If you want to prove you're worthy of promotion and can function beyond your résumé, then work on and promote an idea that no one's attached value to yet, but eventually will. Don't worry if it's something that people may dismiss in the beginning. Do it better than anybody else, and turn a lowly position into a tour de force.

HOT TIP: Couple your dreams with direct strategy. Don't develop the bad habit of following only your passion.

When Pamela's career took off, she looked into her professional crystal ball and saw the Age of Greed. Working for an employment agency, she developed a client base of major corporations such as Celanese, CBS, and Warner-Lambert, and the New York banks, and rightfully anticipated the new wave of stock market baby boomers. She made sure she was on the cutting edge of the eighties Wall Street boom by placing financial and accounting executives.

Mariana Danilovic forecasted a major trend in business. Currently CEO of Digital Media X and a former manager at KPMG's newmedia/Internet practice, she was analyzing business deals at an insurance company when she looked into the future and saw a pot of gold called digital entertainment. So being a woman on the entrepreneurial fast track, Mariana read every article and talked to every person who could teach her anything about the field. She took a lower position at a company in order to hone her skills and show off, and when eventually a man was brought in to head up a low-priority entertainment division (the corporate equivalent of throwing him a bone), our Mariana could smell the opportunity. The poor guy didn't know what hit him. Since they had given him few resources, Mariana volunteered to help out. She would make no more money, but she knew how to leverage a great deal for herself. She would help him in his new division, she said, if he would teach her everything he knew about digital media and technology. Since he was desperate and she was hungry, they struck a deal.

Mariana knew from networking and from reading every piece of research she could find that the then obscure, almost kooky world of e-commerce would eventually explode. She was right. Mariana had morphed into a modern-day seer. An innovator. A pioneer. But not without paying a price. "I learned to be very tenacious. If someone said no, I would just go to another executive and ask the very same question in a different way until they said yes. I just wore people down."

And just in case you need further prodding, here's a cautionary tale: Michelle Kydd, a public relations wunderkind who took her skills to the nonprofit world, was one of those people who simply followed her passion without employing a strategy to go along with it. She had decided early on that she wanted to go into advertising and, without doing much research or networking, moved all the way to Boston from California to pursue her career dream.

On the day she was to start her job search and take over the world, the headline of the *Boston Herald*'s business section read, "Advertising Industry in the Worst Slump Ever." Not much to say after that, is there? Had Michelle stayed on top of the trends, she would have known that her chosen profession was, at that point, in the toilet. "What I learned," Michelle reflects, "was to never set off blindly on a particular course. Take advantage when opportunity knocks. And be ready for opportunity. Whatever it is. Always be aware of what's happening in the marketplace. Be aware of shifts and trends, no matter what you're currently doing. Go ahead and fulfill your passion—but be aware of what's happening in the world around you." We couldn't have said it better ourselves.

## THE SEVENTH COMMANDMENT: *NETWORK*

*New technology may be shrinking our universe down to e-mail, but that doesn't mean you can discount the power of the human relationship.*

Women love to talk. And meet other women. Perhaps one reason behind the tremendous increase in women-owned-

and-operated businesses is that we learned from the women's movement and, before that, from the quilting bees and the coffee klatches that women like to be together on the front lines, helping their communities. And each other.

Our Nadine may not know a quilting bee from a spelling bee, but she sure knows how to network. After becoming a victim of downsizing and burnout during Ted Turner's attempt to take over CBS in the mid-eighties, Nadine wanted to leave television journalism behind and start anew as a producer in the entertainment business. The toughest part of that industry, besides not eating junk food at the craft-services table, is getting in the door. As luck would have it, a former boss had also left television journalism behind and was now running a popular entertainment film and television company. Nadine approached her for help, and her former colleague eagerly put her in touch with her own agent, who in turn got her an interview with Michael Douglas's new entertainment company. Six degrees of separation, but that's networking!

One of the biggest mistakes women make after leaving a professional situation is not keeping in touch with former co-workers. It's tough to do if you were in a job you hated. We know that. No one enjoys looking at a train wreck and reliving the trauma, but it's important to understand that when you leave, you leave behind the company, not the people.

Cynthia Cleveland, president of Universal Studios Consumer Products Group, advises women to stay active in industry groups. "Stay in contact with people. It's a small world. My past associations have always led me to my next path. Never burn bridges. Even where there's conflict, always leave on the best of terms with everyone." (This advice, though sound for careers, does not apply to nightmare ex-boyfriends or husbands.)

"The thing about networking is that it shouldn't end after you get the job," advises Mariana Danilovic. "Networking advances your career. It can definitely help you to get a great job, but it shouldn't end there. In fact, I would say that not keeping up with networking, even when you're successfully hired, is one of the reasons that women on the high end are bumping into the glass ceiling. We're just not networking properly or long enough."

It's true. When you try to change careers, potential employers are likely to do more than check your references. They are going to talk to other industry leaders to get the skinny. After all, if a new organization is going to take a chance on you, then it makes sense that they'll want your contacts and connections as collateral. So make sure you are not only well known in your industry, but thought of as generous and well connected too. As Barbara Dixon says, "I've been a networking person all my life. All of my job moves occurred because of my ability to network. Now I do it even more frequently."

**HOT TIP:** Network from your heart and it will be personally satisfying.

Susan Gordon thinks we network differently as we get older. "Over forty you care about different values. You have a much clearer idea of hierarchy and what contacts can do for you. It's much less about social advancement and more about advancing yourself professionally, more about personal fulfillment."

Denise Jackson thinks we need to reach out more to our younger colleagues. "The power brokers are now our juniors. We need to connect with them and find common ground. With women, common ground is the key. This works across gender, race, and age. Get a clue. Be careful of being parental. It's all about attitude when you network. I project a youthfulness. I am not so serious anymore. We all used to be so serious at forty . . . but the older we get the less that applies. Older is better."

Given that our gender has the reputation of constantly talking, it's surprising that we need to be reminded to network constantly within our own companies. Just because your department is on the sixth floor doesn't mean you're stuck there. Get to know people in other departments. It's a way of forming bonds with people you may work with later. It's also a way of getting a broader view of the company and its larger goals.

You may love your career right now, but you may not love it tomorrow. In order to give yourself as many career options as possible, it's important to be prepared. Now more than ever, women are responsible for inventing their own careers. That means expanding our skills and knowledge. That means branding ourselves as a corporate entity. And more than ever, that means networking.

## The Eighth Commandment: Get a Mentor

*Think mentors are just for kids? You're wrong. Get out there and find someone you admire.*

Guys have the old-boy network. Girls have mentors. It's really important to go out there, find someone you admire, and seek out her nurturing. We all need protection and role-modeling. And whatever your age, it's important to have someone you can talk to honestly, without fear of politicking or recrimination.

Be aware of your peers and your superiors—within your own department and in other departments and divisions within your corporation. Identify, observe, and befriend women whom you admire and feel you can learn from. Which executive women hold positions of power? Who is a great leader of meetings? Who has a reputation for being smart, talented, and a good "people person"? If you have a peer whom you think is smart and sharp, ask her if she currently has a mentor, or if she has ever had a woman influence her over the years. If someone stands out from the crowd, enjoys a reputation of respect, and is on a fast track, make an effort to meet her. Ask to be introduced by someone who may know her. If there is no obvious connection, write a note introducing yourself. Tell her you'd like a brief meeting—say fifteen minutes—to discuss an idea you have. Very few people would refuse that sort of request, especially since you've shown that you are respectful of her time by putting a limit on the meeting. You have something in common—you both work for the same company—so don't be intimidated. She'll have a natural respect and admiration for your aggressiveness. She knows she didn't get anywhere without it! Let your potential mentor know that you admire her skills and would like to know if she would be available to advise you on your career path. Would she be willing to have lunch with you regularly? Let her know that it could be a mutually rewarding relationship. You, of course, would benefit from her wisdom and experience, while she would benefit by learning what is going on in the trenches. Let her know that you can give her access and insight into other areas of the company. Everybody likes to know what's going on.

A mentor can fill you in on the political landscape and advise you how to handle difficult political situations. She can help you make strategic career moves and teach you how to build on your strengths. She can advise you on how to ask for a promotion or a raise and help you determine your worth on the open market.

While you are networking at your industry events, befriend a woman you think you can learn from. Set up lunches or coffee dates, and get to know who's who in your business. A mentor may start out being a business acquaintance who is intermittently helpful on specific issues and end up becoming an integral part of your life on both a personal and professional level.

When Pamela started her career, she was hired by an employment agency that specialized in placing financial executives. New to the game and needing a mentor, she naturally looked to her office mate. He was a mediocre producer with an okay track record. His style was gruff and abrasive. Pamela tried to overlook his idiosyncrasies, even when he inhaled his lunch while conducting business on the telephone. But when the coleslaw drooled out the side of his mouth, Pamela, who doesn't even put salad dressing on her lettuce, knew right there and then that she was never going to learn anything from this man. Frustrated that her style was so at odds with her Oscar Meyer colleague, Pamela asked her boss to put her in an office with the type A high producers so she could learn how to play the game. And she did. Sitting in a room with four top guns day after day, she learned the tricks of the trade, inhaling their skills by osmosis. Minus the pickle breath.

Liz Heller, a former executive vice president of Capitol Records, followed the Sixth Commandment and predicted the new frontier of media technology and its impact on the music industry. So when she sought out a mentor, she looked for someone who could teach her what she needed to know in media, as well as nurture her. Her boss, then at MCA Records, gave her three very useful pieces of advice. First, always take the meeting. You never know who's going to walk through the door with a revolutionary idea. Second, credit is for the bank. Don't worry about who is getting credit for what. A smart boss always sees through the bravado. Just dig in and do the work. And third, make sure you find a mentor who will love you when you're cold. Most corporations or organizations love you when you're hot, so make sure to find a mentor who will see you through the cold and hard times.

Sometimes observing people you don't want to be like can be as important as observing people you admire. Says Michelle Kydd, " I had a female boss in the early eighties who was very competitive with me. It was emotionally very disturbing to the point where I eventually walked away. As a result of that experience, I now mentor every woman I can. For me mentoring is more about giving than receiving. When you build another person's career, you build your own at the same time. The more you serve others, the more resources you'll have. We must learn to share in accolades and accomplishments, to highlight others, and to be grateful. These people whom you mentor will be there to support you during your next transition."

**HOT TIP:** Look beyond the workplace for your mentor.

Mentors can sometimes be found in the home, not the workplace. There are so many people who cultivated us, whom we modeled ourselves after. You have to look at everyone in business as your mentor, see how they behave, how they perform. And each person can help you cross over to shape your own vision. Also look beyond the workplace for your mentor. That person may be a sports coach, your music teacher, your yoga instructor, a religious leader or adviser. Someone with whom you connect in a significant way can have a profound influence on your life.

When Cynthia Cleveland wanted to go into marketing fresh from a teaching career, her first mentor turned out to be someone she barely knew. A step aunt, who showed up at the occasional family gathering and had worked all her life, advised Cynthia to find a company with a built-in management training program, and commanded her, no matter what, not to take any job where her job description was *secretary*. "Take less money," she advised. "But never take that title. You'll never shake it."

Renée Fraser's best mentor, a woman by the name of Mary Wells—one of the first women in advertising (Wells, Rich, Green)—taught her to be very visible in her job and to merchandise the hell out of herself. "She taught me to let my personality drive my career, to be who I am, and to never be afraid or embarrassed to take the spotlight."

Diane Krouse, who runs DMB&B Agency in Los Angeles, cites her mother as her greatest mentor. "She had been an extremely beautiful Copacabana showgirl. But one of my earliest memories of my mother was of her sitting on the kitchen floor taking apart a broken toaster. Watching my mother do something that was traditionally male, and do it with such authority and success, gave me the feeling that I, too, could do anything. My mother didn't go out and make a living, but she role-modeled the worth of accomplishment and independence on a daily basis." Let's all take a moment.

# THE NINTH COMMANDMENT: VOLUNTEER

*Not everything you do is meant to last forever. That's why God invented dating before marriage, the henna tattoo, and volunteer jobs.*

It's important to understand that volunteering no longer means candy-striping. Our world thrives because of the endless amount of effort and time that women put into charitable work at hospitals, fund-raisers, and PTAs. But there's no law against using volunteering to help yourself while you're helping others.

It behooves you to try on a new career the same way you'd try on a dress. A dress may look good on the rack, but it may not have the same allure once you try it on. So, too, with a career. Involving yourself in a world you think you want to be a part of is a productive way to separate reality from fantasy. And while no one may hire you for your newly chosen field right away, there are bound to be organizations that would value your skills while you're building your résumé. Find them.

Michelle Kydd, now the co-executive director of the foundation at Creative Artist Agency, believes volunteering is the best way to try out new careers. You won't get stuck (or go broke) and can educate and prepare yourself for a career that sounds great on paper but may not be what you actually want to do twelve hours a day. Volunteering gives you the opportunity to check out the reality of your dream job. You discover the day-to-day responsibilities, the necessary skills, and the time demands. And it allows you to fill in the blanks. Pamela has heard from countless women who want to enter the public relations field because they love people, but have no idea that half the job entails writing. Volunteering lets you ask questions, and what you learn will help you make the right career choice. And it gives you valuable experience.

In 1978, while working as a part-time psychologist, Nadine wanted to enter television journalism. But without a tape that demonstrated her interviewing skills in front of a camera she couldn't get her foot in the door. Therein lay the catch-22. Without a demo tape she couldn't even cold call for an interview, but without an interview, how would she get on tape? Nadine needed concrete evidence that she could interview people and be presentable on camera. So she called the manager of her local cable station and made a deal. Nadine would use her experience as a therapist to fill in thirty minutes of airtime with an on-air interview session, and in return the station would give her a complimentary reel of her show. The station manager was thrilled to hear from a potential contributor who was not a psychic or a yoga instructor, but a professional interested in hosting a cable access program using her psychology background. It was perfect. Nadine decided to base her interview on the topic of phobias and enlisted her good friend Marion, who happened to have a terrible fear of flying. She and Marion went before the camera, and Nadine pointed out all the different ways this phobia could be treated. Before the interview Nadine asked the studio technician which way to look, what the blinking light was for, and what his hand signals meant as he counted her down and off the air. And now she understood what it meant to "wrap." In the end, she had a great half-hour tape to show of herself as an interviewer, and the cable outlet filled a half hours' worth of time with someone not wearing bell-bottoms. Unfortunately, and she still feels a little bad about this, Marion was left with her fear of flying. But, like a good friend, she was happy for Nadine and insisted she was happy taking the bus.

# TENTH COMMANDMENT: *DON'T LET THE BASTARDS GET YOU DOWN*

*Don't forget who you are and what you're made of. Navigate past the bastards and their obstacles. There will be many.*

Chivalry isn't dead. It just never existed in the workplace. So, if you're waiting for someone to roll out that red carpet by the elevator or for some white knight to deliver the glass slipper to your desk . . . boy, have you been ordering from the wrong deli.

Margaret Loesch, a prime-time mover and shaker in the television business, had an early experience in her career that helped build her character. All thanks to a bastard. When she was first starting out with NBC as a junior executive, she and her boss went up to the penthouse suite to pitch their ideas to a head honcho we'll refer to as the big man. Margaret's boss asked her to begin the presentation, and while she spoke, the big man got up from his desk and started pacing around the room. Undeterred, Margaret gamely paced behind him, not missing a beat. At one point the big man was so engrossed with his own story notes he was unaware he had not closed the door while peeing. Margaret, to her credit, turned her back and looked out over the Rockefeller Center skating rink and kept up the conversation while her boss sat in horror. After the big man zipped up, he put his arm around her and told her she'd done a fine job. That coolness under pressure, that ability to get the job done, was the experience that helped develop her reputation. From then on, she became known as the woman who could do anything, the personification of grace under fire. As bizarre as it was, pitching the upcoming pilot season under stressful circumstances made her name, and her career.

Linda Lytle knows all about the bastards. "When I started, it was both a privilege and a nightmare to be the first female in a senior management position. There was a good-old-boy mentality where everyone thought it was funny to bring a stripper in for lunch. There was one older guy who would always come up to me and say, 'Congratulations.' He said it habitually, every time I saw him. I never knew why. Years later, when I left the company, I finally asked him. He told me the guys in the office had a pool as to whom I would sleep with first. And since I never slept with any of them, he always said congratulations to me for outsmarting their chauvinism."

Cynthia Cleveland attributes her professional success to a guy who tried to keep her down. A male coworker took to blowing cigar smoke in her face, not to mention slapping her on the back while dishing out backhanded compliments. A master of passive-aggressive behavior, he told Cynthia that she would be the first woman to make it to management in the next five years. Rather than giving her hope, the comment hit her like a bucket of cold water. Cynthia realized he was right. It took the guys three years to move up the corporate ladder. It would take her five. And she didn't have five years to wait until her next promotion. Much to the amazement of Mr. Insensitive, she quit that day. And refused to let the bastards get her down.

# Chapter Three

# Unzip Yourself: How to Change Your Career

## Define Your Passion

"You can't go to a passion store. So how do you find your passion? It's hard. You're unhappy in your work. You're depressed. You can't get out of bed. You cry. You don't exercise. But you do whatever it takes, 'cause change is wonderful." So says Fran Pomeranz, a forty-eight-year-old woman with a background in restaurant management who changed careers in her forties. Fran knew she wanted to make a change, but she didn't know where to start. "I was at the same company for years and had reached all of my goals, not to mention the pinnacle of my learning curve. How was I supposed to know what to do next?"

The first step in answering the question "What do I want to do?" is to identify your interests and your passions. Establish your own set of values. Take a piece of paper and draw a line down the center. List the things you *love* to do on one side and the things you *hate* to do on the other. Be very specific. Include intangible items like: I love to be with my friends; or, I want to be Greta Garbo and work alone. Do you like teamwork? Taking pictures? Reading history? Organizing your closet? No way. You like organizing your closet? You just lost a standing invitation to either one of our own homes.

Now be very general. Think about all the careers in which you've ever had an interest. Think of the job titles and all that you associate with them. Recall your dreams and ambitions—those you let slip away, those you still entertain. You're over thirty-five now. Chances are you have the resources to pursue one of those dreams and ignite one of those passions. You're at a great point in your life. You have experience behind you and opportunity in front of you. You may not be a wunderkind, but neither are you ready for the early-bird special. You've learned from your mistakes and are ready to make a big change. So examine your lists, connect them. What is there in your list of "loves" and "hates" that relates to your dream job list? Evaluate the connections and the discrepancies. If you said that you hate performing, but listed *tap dancer* as a dream job, well, that's one you should consider dismissing. Likewise, if you've said that you always wanted to be a writer and listed "love to play with words" in your list, that's something to pay attention to.

An investment adviser would tell you to evaluate your assets and diversify your investments for maximum return. Good advice. And now that you're investing in yourself, the same applies. Evaluate your assets—in this case your skills, your time, and your money—and consider how best to diversify them. That means thinking about the big picture. Realistically. Every career description has a big heading with all the responsibilities listed underneath. You probably have an idea of the big heading you're interested in, but you need to do some work to find out what all those day-to-day responsibilities are. You owe it to yourself to find out what's behind the dream. Talk to people. Research. You may think you have a grand passion for the big picture, but until you know the underlying value system—until you know what goes on beyond the salary and the hype—you won't know if that career is right for you.

# THE A–Z KNOW-THYSELF GUIDE TO CHANGING CAREERS

Our lives have become so frenetic and fast-paced. We are so busy trying to juggle all our responsibilities and interests that we forget to take contemplative moments. Now is the time for you to reflect upon yourself. How can you make a change if you don't know what's important to you? And how can you know—*really know*—what's important to you if you don't take the time to reflect? Refer to the following guide often. It's a valuable tool and will help you whenever you feel the need to reassess. Be totally honest with yourself, and enjoy the journey.

**A.** Are you feeling out of sync with yourself? Things out of whack? Have your eating habits changed? Are you stuffing yourself or starving? Are you being harsh with the kids or snapping at your spouse or partner? Are you tired when normally you've got energy to burn? Then something's wrong and you need to take a look at yourself.

**B.** Admit your fears. Embarking on a new career can activate all those old insecurities. After all, you are putting yourself in a vulnerable position, and no one likes to be judged. So go ahead. Admit your fears. You'll never get past them if you don't know what they are. But don't be harsh on yourself. We're all scared of failing.

**C.** Think about your childhood. Did you feel supported by your parents? Did they encourage and challenge you? Were you forever looking for their approval? Our earliest relationships are often our most important, so be candid with yourself. When you were growing up, did you look up to your father or mother as a role model? Did you admire them? Or did they show you how *not* to live your life? Negative role models are often more powerful than positive ones, so give this some thought. And don't forget to factor your siblings into the equation. Family hierarchy and sibling rivalry have a huge impact on your success in life.

**D.** Think about why you chose the career path you are currently on. There are multiple factors to consider—money, intellectual stimulation, an influential role model, an early mentor or hero. Or did your career choose you? If so, what were the circumstances?

**E.** Does your present career afford you the time to satisfy other important needs? Are you working too hard? Do you have enough time for family and friends? Think about what may be pulling at you—your mothering responsibilities, your desire to play the electric guitar or improve your tennis game. That sort of thing.

**F.** Develop a wish list. Start with now, then three-to-five years from now, and ten years. Fantasize. Dream. Let your thoughts flow freely, and write it all down.

**G.** Assess what aspect of your work you like the most and find the most satisfying. Be specific.

**H.** List the aspects of your current job that are your least favorite. Don't like the people? Don't like the location? Don't like your boss? Be clear and be honest. Write it all down, even if some things seem petty or unimportant.

**I.** Think about how other people see you. Step outside yourself and think about what your superiors, your peers, and your subordinates might say if they had to describe you. Think about your reputation in your field. Does it make you proud—or is there room for some improvement?

**J.** List all of your personal strengths. Are you a conceptional thinker (someone who thinks big and is a creative thinker), or a linear thinker (someone who thinks in a logical step-by-step process)? Do you have a sense of humor? How are your organizational skills? Are you tenacious, intelligent, and ambitious?

**K.** List all of your weaknesses. (Chocolate, anyone?)

L. If you have a temper, think about what triggers it. What really annoys you? Someone driving really slowly in front of you, or maybe someone who doesn't think as quickly as you do?

M. List your best work scenarios. Where do you feel most happy and satisfied?

N. Some of us need structure. Some of us hate it. What arena do you thrive in? Are you happiest in the womb of a large company with all of its concomitant support systems? Or would you prefer the free-wheeling, unstructured environment of an entrepreneurial start-up?

O. Be honest. Is the glass half full or half empty? Be aware of how you wake up in the morning. Are you excited and enthused about the new day, or do you feel weighted down? Which is more you: "the optimist" or "the pessimist"?

P. List your greatest professional accomplishments. What was your proudest professional moment?

Q. List your personal accomplishments. What was your proudest personal moment?

R. List the five key priorities in your life. Don't distinguish between personal and professional.

S. Try to define your talents—those gifts that are your natural abilities doled out at birth, and those that you developed through training and practice.

T. Think about the daily scenarios (chores, the market, the dry cleaner, PTA, charity) in which you use "business" skills—for example, leading, persuading, mentoring, or training.

U. Recognize your ability to inspire. List examples.

V. When do you perform best? As a leader, a strong number two, or part of a team?

W. Think about women you admire. What traits do they have that you'd like to emulate? Being a copycat can be a good thing, you know.

X. People who play sports are often high achievers. What sports did you play in your high school and college days? If you didn't play sports, what held you back?

Y. It is very important to surround yourself with people who nurture you. Who serves as your support system?

Z. Imagine your ultimate fantasy job. Let your mind go wild. What would be the absolute greatest? Is it managing a bed and breakfast in New England or working on a cruise ship in the Bahamas?

## AS OTHERS SEE YOU

Other people often see things about you that you don't see yourself. That can be terrifying, but it can be useful too. Take the plunge and ask colleagues, peers, and mentors what they honestly think about you—what they really and sincerely think. Instruct them to be forthright and specific. Stand by with tissues, chocolate bars, and some great rented movies that you've always wanted to see. Just in case. Try this exercise with a friend or family member. More than one, if you can muster the courage. You may learn things about yourself that refer to the core value system we spoke of earlier. Consider their feedback a gift that will help you reinvent yourself without going to a therapist. Do not under any circumstances try this exercise with your mother. In that particular case, feedback may seem more intense and therefore more important than it is.

Here are some sample questions to get you started:

- Am I a good listener?
- Am I able to assess a situation with clarity?
- Do I look you in the eye when I talk to you?
- How have I handled criticism in our relationship?
- Do you think I am capable of managing a staff?
- Do I have compassion and understanding?
- Am I committed to completing a task?

The inventory of your strengths and weaknesses is your key to self-knowledge and should give you an idea of what, in particular, you bring to the table. Once you know, don't depend on anybody else to sell you, not even an executive recruiter. An executive recruiter's main interest is in filling a particular position for a corporation. Often they think only to place a square peg into a square opening or a round peg into a round opening. You need to *inspire* a recruiter to think outside of the box. Pamela says, "There are often times when I'll interview a candidate whose skill sets may not be one hundred percent of what my client wants, but her personality, verbal ability, and intelligence are so impressive that I'll present her to my client and convince the executive to meet her." Ultimately it is up to you to generate the excitement and interest to create the scenario in which you can showcase yourself. Don't rely on anyone to do it for you. You are the head of your own marketing and advertising division. So go run the campaign of your life!

Making change and taking charge requires a process of self-evaluation. If you want to take a risk and change careers, you need to know yourself and, more important, believe in yourself. A career makeover is life-altering—not something you want to do every few years. You'll need to know your personality and character attributes, your priorities, and your goals in order to do so successfully. The Unzip Yourself Test will help you evaluate yourself. It will help you determine whether you actually need a makeover and, if so, what direction that makeover should take. Go to it!

## Unzip Yourself Test

1. At the last minute your immediate supervisor asks you to rewrite the report you have been working on for weeks. Furious and exhausted, you
   a. show your anger, but petulantly go back to the drawing board.

b. ask for an explanation of what is missing and why it took her so long to respond.

c. agree to revise it immediately with no hesitation.

2. You are job hunting and have three offers in your field. You accept the job that offers
a. the most money.
b. flextime and a lower salary.
c. a fast track and competitive environment.

3. Your boss has just been promoted and wants to take you with her. Flattered, you
a. tell her you need three days to think it over.
b. jump at the opportunity.
c. question her about the additional workload and day-to-day responsibilities.

4. Upon overhearing a conversation about a brand-new product launch, you
a. immediately approach your boss to volunteer for the project.
b. think it's a fabulous idea, but really, you have no extra time for it.
c. wonder whether your marketing skills are good enough to accept the challenge.

5. A colleague invites you to hear a panel of experts talk about the future of telecommunications, but you have a prior personal engagement. You

a. accept gladly and cancel the prior appointment.

b. tell her that you have no interest in telecommunications—you are currently in fashion.

c. decline the invitation. You have a hot date with a new guy.

6. You have a business convention in Las Vegas—the biggest yearly function for your industry—and your son's soccer final is that same weekend. You

a. arrange for your husband to be *supermom* and go to the game for both of you.

b. prepare your subordinate to go to the convention in your place.

c. feel the convention is inconsequential. You know most of the attendees—and there's always next year.

7. You have been at the same company for seven years and now have an opportunity to take a six-month sabbatical. You would

a. join your husband or partner and take that long-awaited trip to Africa.

b. begin that novel you've always dreamed of writing.

c. pass on the opportunity because you're on such a fast track.

8. All of your friends are on-line. You feel like a dinosaur because your computer skills are rusty. You

a. say to yourself: *So what if I'm not a techie. That field doesn't really interest me, anyway.*

b. enroll in a night class to learn the necessary skills.

c. invite your friends to your home for a "computer party" to share expertise and stories—giving you incentive and support.

9. A woman for whom you have a high regard is the creative director of your company. You work in accounting. You

a. admire her from afar. You two are in different fields—you'd have nothing in common.

b. call her and introduce yourself, then invite her to lunch.

c. find someone you know in your company to introduce you.

10. A client with whom you've done business has just told you he gave an important assignment to one of your key competitors, *who just happens to be a guy*. You

a. understand that he may need to spread the wealth around.

b. ask him if he thinks your company has not performed up to par and request a personal meeting to discuss the current situation.

c. shrug. You win some. You lose some. That's business.

11. Two of your colleagues have a serious difference of opinion on an approach to a new business presentation. It is causing serious conflict and disruption. You

a. stay out of it. It could be bad politically.

b. ask them both to meet with you to try and mediate the situation.

    c. align yourself with the individual who shares your opinion.

12. Your close girlfriend calls and suggests you take a film class one night a week for six weeks. You
    a. decline immediately because you want your evenings free for business events.
    b. tell her you'll mull it over. You generally try to be home at night for the kids.
    c. think it's a fabulous idea. You, love film and this would be a real kick.

13. Invited by a friend to her company's holiday party, you
    a. decline. You hate these types of gatherings—everyone eats and drinks too much.
    b. jump at the chance! It's a great networking opportunity.
    c. politely say no. Your own holiday party is enough.

14. You hear from a colleague that a competing publishing house is paying $10,500 more per year for the same job you hold. You
    a. go directly to your boss's office and ask for a raise.
    b. think about putting yourself on the market.
    c. don't care. You love your work.

15. Your husband, partner, or friend wants you to join him or her for an extreme-sport experience—six lessons, then a rock-climbing excursion to the High Sierras. You
    a. say matter-of-factly that you'll think about it—but say to yourself, *No way!*

b. say you'd love to go, but can't. You have a load of work and a presentation to prepare.

c. absolutely go! This is a once-in-a-lifetime opportunity.

16. If you could choose an additional project at work to advance skills, you would
    a. do a focus group with teenage girls for a cosmetics company.
    b. assist in a strategic-marketing and financial plan for a media acquisition.
    c. write a press release about your company's newest high-tech software application.

17. If you had an evening free, you would choose to
    a. play bridge or Scrabble with friends.
    b. go to the opera with your husband, partner, or friend.
    c. stay home and read a good book.

18. If you were having difficulty solving a problem at work, you would
    a. do the research yourself—it's quicker to find the answer that way.
    b. discuss it with a colleague. She might come up with another angle.
    c. immediately go to your boss and ask for help.

19. One of your close friends is a member of a nonprofit inner-city charity that supports at-risk, low-income

teenagers in after-school mentoring programs. She invites you to become a member of her fund-raising committee. You

a. are thrilled to participate. You've been looking for a way to give back to those less fortunate.

b. refuse her overture. You're really busy with your career and don't need any distractions.

c. tell her you'd like to think about it—after all, it might be a good networking opportunity!

20. You want to change careers. You feel restless, bored, and *been there, done that.* You

a. tell all your friends and discuss it with them.

b. quit your job and think about what's next.

c. begin to explore all resources available

## Answers for Scoring

| | | |
|---|---|---|
| 1. a. = 0 | 5. a. = 3 | 9. a. = 0 |
| b. = 3 | b. = 1 | b. = 3 |
| c. = 3 | c. = 1 | c. = 2 |
| 2. a. = 0 | 6. a. = 3 | 10. a. = 1 |
| b. = 2 | b. = 2 | b. = 3 |
| c. = 3 | c. = 1 | c. = 1 |
| 3. a. = 0 | 7. a. = 2 | 11. a. = 3 |
| b. = 3 | b. = 2 | b. = 2 |
| c. = 2 | c. = 3 | c. = 1 |
| 4. a. = 3 | 8. a. = 1 | 12. a. = 3 |
| b. = 1 | b. = 3 | b. = 2 |
| c. = 0 | c. = 2 | c. = 2 |

13. a. = 0
    b. = 3
    c. = 2
14. a. = 3
    b. = 1
    c. = 2
15. a. = 0
    b. = 3

    c. = 2
16. a. = 2
    b. = 3
    c. = 1
17. a. = 2
    b. = 2
    c. = 2
18. a. = 3

    b. = 1
    c. = 2
19. a. = 2
    b. = 3
    c. = 2
20. a. = 2
    b. = 0
    c. = 3

## If You Scored 48–59 Points:

You demonstrate tremendous ambition and a strong desire for personal growth. You are ready to make work and career the top priority in your life, and are willing to realign other areas such as family and hobbies. You are adept at networking and tracking trends inside and outside your field—a must for any career change. Although generally not engaged in company politics, you tend to confront issues head-on, with honesty and directness. You are forthright, but sometimes you act impulsively, and this impulsiveness may need to be checked. You tend to be competitive—with yourself and others. Success to you is both monetary and material. You have a desire for excellence and continued personal growth, and are always seeking to improve your natural talents. Do make sure, though, that in your quest for self-improvement you don't forget to appreciate your already considerable skills and experience. And do make sure that you keep a close check on those who are important to you. You are so focused on career right now that it would be easy to neglect family and friends, but never forget that you need them as much as they need you.

Take a deep breath, and consider carefully the consequences of your actions. (Yes, actions do have consequences. . . .) Be careful not to step on too many toes on your climb up the ladder. Relationships are one of the keys to a successful business career, so be careful to find positive ways of channeling your competitiveness. Don't get us wrong: competitiveness is a good thing. And we're certainly not suggesting you return to the "good girl" role. Just be careful not to burn bridges in your enthusiasm and eagerness to "get there" and achieve.

Work is the most fulfilling part of your life right now, so this is a wonderful time for you to undergo a career makeover. You have the energy and drive to succeed in your commitment to change. The sky's the limit!

## *If You Scored 27–47 Points:*

Success is important to you, but not at any price. You have a need to create a balanced life between work and family, a desire to nurture yourself and others. You are ambitious, but loyalty and devotion temper your ambition. You would never take a job just for more money. Quality of work is of paramount importance to you. Keep this in mind as you consider your makeover.

Moderation is key. You are dedicated to your work, but need to make room for play. You enjoy indulging in life's pleasures. You have outside interests and want to keep them. You pride yourself on your relationships and use your professional and personal network to bring people together—not just for your own purposes. Generally a team player, you have a generosity of spirit that is admired by many. Make sure, though, that you save some of that generosity for yourself. Make a point of promoting yourself—especially now. Don't downplay your accomplishments, and don't shrink from using those networks for your own benefit. You'd be surprised at how many people you have come in contact with in your professional and personal life. Take stock and make contact.

Be sure to consider a flexible work schedule when planning your new career. Review your future employer's human resources policy. Is it family friendly? Does it allow for family commitments and honor personal time? You are a prime candidate for telecommuting, so consider that option when shopping around your considerable skills. Technology is changing the geography of the workplace; there has never been a better time to work from home. And if you've ever thought of starting your own business . . . perhaps now's the time to take the plunge!

## If You Scored 1–26 Points:

You're stuck. You feel insecure about your abilities. You shy away from promoting yourself and tend to be humble about your achievements. Constantly comparing yourself to others, you feel inadequate and often apprehensive. You may be a very talented and capable woman, but you are your own worst enemy.

Your career path is not defined. Still searching for the "right" approach, you have let fear get in your way. Chances are you've accomplished a lot more than you give yourself credit for. Recall these accomplishments—objectively. Be realistic about what you have achieved in the past, and use those achievements to take stock of yourself. Be sensible and take your time. Work through our *Know Thyself, A–Z Guide to Changing Careers,* and pay special attention to *Seven Steps to Getting Unstuck.* Take your time, and don't be too hard on yourself. That never got anybody anywhere.

Learn to be proactive instead of reactive. Create some quiet time for yourself and evaluate your behavior. Understand that you *can* have a satisfying career. You may not realize it, but you've been acting like a victim. That has got to stop. Explore therapy and self-help organizations. Investigate support groups and start to network. Take baby steps. Build your self-esteem. You don't need to be perfect, but you do need to take that first step. Remember: It all begins with you.

## GETTING UNSTUCK

It is truly one of life's cruel ironies that even when we're bored, dissatisfied, and stuck in a job that offers us little joy or challenge, we hold on to it because that's preferable to dealing with our fear of the unknown. Guess what? The clock is ticking, and you will never know the pleasure of work you love to do if you keep resisting what life may have to offer. If you don't have time to read this book in its entirety, but need to get started on "letting go," we suggest you follow these seven steps to getting unstuck. *All together now: Time to get unattached. Disconnected. Unfastened. Defused. Unglued. And dislodged.* Congratulations. You are now entering the free-fall space of a totally new career. Houston we have a problem. And you are about to get a fast solution.

## Seven Steps to Getting Unstuck

• **List everything that interests you.** Sit down and let your imagination run wild. Include your vocation and avocations. What strikes your fancy? Visit a newsstand and look at the variety of magazines. Study the ads in the back. Do any of these opportunities match anything you want to do?

• **List your skill sets.** If you are presently working, break down all aspects of your job. Be specific. If you're on a career hiatus, what about volunteer experience or your day-to-day tasks? You'll be surprised at how many of them are business related. It's important to acknowledge your skills. All of them.

• **Think about what you really love doing.** These should be actual tasks, whether work related or not. Consider those activities in which you are currently engaged, and those that have occupied you in the past. Which ones did you love, *really* love? Go way back. Is there anything that you've let go of that perhaps you'd like to pick up again?

• **Research companies that interest you.** Begin by thinking about your passions. Are you crazy about lipstick? Do you harbor a shoe fetish? Do you yearn to travel, or would you be happier nestled in the stacks of a bookstore? What companies are engaged in these businesses? What companies do you think would stimulate your mind and satisfy your desires? Cross-reference these companies with your personal network of contacts. Go on. What are you waiting for?

- **Read! read! read!** Read trade magazines, business journals, *all* the newspapers. And not just print. Read on-line too. Reading will keep you current and inspire you. Information is a fabulous currency.

- **Take classes.** Contact your local university and see what classes they offer. These classes can broaden your horizons, and they can also turn out to be valuable networking opportunities. Very often the professor of the class will be a business executive. Make yourself known to her.

- **Volunteer.** Get involved in politics, charities, the arts. Volunteering is a great way to expand your network of people and a great way to learn about new opportunities, both business and social. Volunteering can help you make your own opportunities.

# WANDA G.——CAREER MAKEOVER

When Wanda came to see us, she was going through a difficult transition in her life. The bank where she had worked for the last ten years was merging with Deutsche Bank, and her position was being eliminated. In truth, Wanda had known for some time that her days in the banking business were numbered. Frustrated with her losing battle to move into the upper ranks of investment management, she was coming to terms with the fact that banking is largely East Coast based—

not to mention clubby. Very few African-American women have gained entrance into the upper echelons of banking, so even though Wanda was afraid of losing her benefits and a steady paycheck, she viewed being downsized as a way to recharge her career and take off in a different direction.

Wanda had graduated from the University of Southern California with an MBA in finance. She began her banking career in 1983 as operations officer at Bank of America, organizing, developing, and training staff in customer relations, as well as coordinating personnel and supervising workflow and salary administration. After four years in this position she moved on to the Bankers Trust Company, where she began her ten-year career. Starting as an investment assistant, she processed fixed-income, equity, and global trade settlements for institutional accounts. She dealt with brokers, consultants, and investment managers in corporations and foundations, managing and administering their multibillion-dollar portfolios of pension retirement funds.

In addition to her Fortune 500 corporate client base, Wanda managed funds for nonprofit organizations that gave money to charitable causes. She liked her involvement with these socially responsible entities. She liked the feeling that came with helping others. It was this experience that led Wanda to think she should become more involved with the nonprofits by managing their money directly. Wanda knew from talking to her agency clients that they seldom hired a professional to handle their financial affairs in-house. Still, she thought her background in tax and accounting could be of great value to them. Since it was her job to police the managers who were actually investing the money, Wanda knew that the funds could use tighter controls. When it came to going global with international funds, for instance, there were a lot of risks, especially when investing in under-developed countries. Wanda wanted to be the one to manage those risks.

We began Wanda's job search by having her list all of the nonprofit foundations she had come in contact with over the years. The work in which Wanda was interested involved being on the opposite side of the desk from where she had sat for over decade, so we suggested she draw up a detailed inventory of all the agency people she knew, with notes that included their titles and the nature of their agency involvement. This proved to be a vast and invaluable resource.

Next we looked at Wanda's résumé. She had an excellent base résumé, but she needed to tailor it to meet her new goals. She needed to show how she could leverage her skills and banking know-how into the nonprofit world. We recommended Wanda format her new résumé to highlight her foundation experience. She listed each foundation separately, defining what she did for each one. That allowed her to articulate her nonprofit experience, which was actually quite extensive. Her financial skills were strong—so strong that no one would question them—but now the foundations could understand how those financial skills could be applied directly to them. Yes, she had worked for banks, but her day-to-day experience was with her clients, the foundations.

Wanda's next task was to write a brief cover letter indicating her extensive banking experience and her familiarity with the specific needs of the foundation to which she was applying. In order to let a potential employer know she was well-connected, we advised her to mention the names of one or two of the executives she knew who would sing her praises. Wanda had also expressed a desire to share some of her ideas that she thought would benefit the foundations, so we suggested a cover letter that would include a proactive analysis-solutions approach that would take advantage of her intimate knowledge of the nonprofit world. Armed with insider information from her banking days, she included in her cover letter a brief analysis of some of the problems she knew existed between the foundations and the bank. She then listed several solutions to the problems, which ensured that her follow-up phone calls and e-mails would be answered.

Wanda had savvy and know-how. She had fourteen years of experience in banking, ten years of contact with foundation staff, and a passion for nonprofit work. And she introduced herself as a problem solver. Who wouldn't want her on their team? Wanda felt better about her job search with our support behind her. Just having someone on her side made her feel more confident, she said. But before the foundations started clamoring to meet Wanda, we wanted her to update her look. Wanda had just had a baby, which, as we all know, eliminates all time for self-maintenance. Nevertheless, it didn't take much to persuade her that touch-ups and cosmetics were not a luxury when you're searching for a new career. The update didn't take long. In just under four hours, a hairdresser and makeup person gave Wanda just the look she needed: a new do and easy regime that left her feeling attractive and very confident. Time well spent.

The first couple of interview experiences gave Wanda some insight. An executive recruiter called for a position as a risk-management analyst at an investment trust company that dealt with global issues. It wasn't exactly the nonprofit world Wanda was hoping for, but wanting to get herself out there, she met with the director of human resources. "I met with him for an hour or so," she said. "The questions he asked me were very technical. In terms of interview style, he was very dry, giving me one-word answers to my questions about the company. At the end of the interview, he told me that he didn't think I would fit with the manager of the department, that our styles weren't compatible. My recruiter later told me that the particular manager wanted a more aggressive personality. I don't consider myself an aggressive person, but I am assertive. If the recruiter had said I wasn't assertive enough, then I'd need to think about how I presented my skills. But on the whole, for my first time out, I felt good about my interview."

Wanda then interviewed for a community-relations position with a major insurance conglomerate in California. She passed the first interview with the director of human resources, and then went in to see the director of the department. Wanda recalls every detail. "He had the great corner office with a great view of the city and a huge picture of Yankee Stadium on one wall. You knew this guy was from New York and loved it because the signs were all over his office." During their interview, he referred to the fact that there was a possibility of training for this position in New York City. "I realize now I should have told him how exciting that would be and how much I loved the Yankees. Instead I was kind of blasé, which I'm sure gave him the impression I hated the city. I have worked in New York, and it's not really my kind of

77

town, but I realize now I should have just bitten the bullet, recognized all the signs around me, and told him I'd be delighted to spend some time in the Big Apple. I ignored all the personal cues that speak to an interviewer's hobbies and interests. I'll never make that mistake again."

After that, Wanda got a lead for the Salvation Army by networking with a former colleague. Not only did she get an interview, her timing was impeccable. They had interviewed many candidates, none of whom was right for the job. But Wanda bowled them over with her knowledge of their business and her professional presentation. Her years of working with foundations gave them the background they needed, and they offered her the job of assistant director of trust services for their planned-giving department. Wanda was ecstatic. Finally she would be able to marry her avocation with her vocation, be spiritually satisfied *and* make money. All at the same time!

**Epilogue:** Six months after Wanda was hired at the Salvation Army, a change in management occurred and the new major wanted to install his own corpsman to take over Wanda's position. Not wanting to take their final offer of a position a notch down the food chain, she decided to leave. The experience with the Salvation Army made Wanda aware of the similarities between the corporate and nonprofit worlds. Just because you are doing work that helps other people doesn't mean the people running the foundation are going to be benevolent or operate from their hearts when it comes to employees. Explains Wanda, "The Salvation Army turned out to be a church organization with a large management structure. All of the senior managers were members of the Army of the Universal Church. It was either Major this, or Colonel that. What I thought it would be like in terms of a working environment turned out to be quite different when I got inside. It was similar to the bank in that senior management in the corporate world is generally older men who have been in the military. And that military mentality is everywhere in the culture. Now I will research an organization's corporate culture before I accept a position . . . with a fine-tooth comb."

Wanda is doing well. She is more comfortable and more confident than before, and tells us that leaving the company she'd been at for years was a kind of testing ground for her. She is still interested in foundation work, but her stint at the Salvation Army made her realize that she wants to create more of a balance between her personal and professional life. And that balance will be a priority in the next job she goes after. What started out as anxiety from the downsizing has turned into a desire for a life of inner peace and satisfaction.

## ROBIN GROTH—CAREER MAKEOVER

When we first met with Robin, she had, at age fifty-two, already had a successful twenty-five-year career as a network television producer and on-air correspondent. She came to us because her production unit at CNN had been shut down in a company downsizing, and the network's plan to put her on a new women's network had been shelved.

Robin's fantasy was to become an international correspondent, focusing on what she calls "cultural exploration."

She had already worked for World Vision filming documentaries and had not ruled out relocating from Los Angeles to become a freelance war correspondent. She was also toying with the possibility of engaging in one of her main loves and traveling to remote areas to visually document indigenous people, perhaps also exploring her interest in alternative health and medicine.

Robin was at a crossroads. Should she continue her journalism career through the television networks or use her skills to pursue other areas? On-air television becomes difficult for women as they age. Robin knew the cold, hard facts. And television producing, with its deadlines and travel, requires great physical and mental stamina. How long should Robin hang in? And given how much she loves reporting, why should she have to give it up?

Robin saw her strengths as being able to weave a story and make everyone, from a CEO in New York to a stranger in Africa, comfortable talking to her. She was no longer interested in the pressure that comes from having to write a story in a day, no longer interested in crafting a news piece and turning a phrase in a crash-and-burn (that's a late-breaking news story to you and me). She did, however, want to continue to make her yearly base salary of approximately one hundred and fifty thousand dollars a year. And who could blame her?

We listened to Robin and assessed her situation. Could she marry her passion to her vocation and continue in the world of journalism on her own terms? Was it possible for her to take her considerable, hard-earned journalistic skills and transfer them to a new job or career without having to start from scratch? We asked Robin to share her career transition journey with us:

"If I were to describe a dream job, it would be a job where I could get paid for what I love. So if you're asking me, 'If I could do anything, what would it be?' I would say that it would be to work with a corporation that had just moved into new offices and had a global interest in, basically, saving the world . . . and that there would be somebody within that company who was too busy themselves to go out and see the world, so they would send me." That sure sounds like a dream job, but we did ask.

"Network television can be extremely backbiting, extremely aggressive, and critical. I've been there. Done that. I've survived that overly competitive world. Now I would like to move on to something else. I think competition is wonderful when you elevate everybody, when you take everyone along and say, 'Hey, it wasn't just me, it was the team.' I sound like I'm getting an Oscar here, but it's true. That's how I feel. Competition becomes a problem when you have an executive who pits people against each other because [he thinks] that's the way to get people to work better. There was too much of that in network television. Far too much.

"When our department at CNN was eliminated, a lot of us were very upset. We were told that we would have jobs equal or better somewhere in the Time Warner family. But Time Warner is a huge organization, and there were seventeen people in my unit laid off, all of whom have excellent credentials. If the brass really meant what they were saying, all of us would have been placed internally at either HBO or Telepictures [Time Warner subsidiaries]. So why were we sending out our résumés?

"As broadcast cultures go, CNN is one of the best. But it's still, as one of my colleagues puts it, 'crabs in a barrel.' There's fear. Absolute fear. And I don't like being in a place where people rule by fear or criticism. I'm over it. I'm through. It's not the way I deal with people. I think I'm a kind person who helps others when they have problems, probably to a fault. I try to include people and help them feel they're always part of a team. I've changed as I've gotten older. I used to like to control everything around me, but now I try to delegate. I'm doing much better at that.

"So, I've been exploring television possibilities, minus the corporate culture I don't like. For example, right now I'm looking into Discovery and National Geographic for their long-form content. There's a new network called the American Health Network, although I'm not really clear on what they intend to do and how soon. Another fantasy of mine is to host A&E's *Biography*. But my dream would be to combine my television reporting and producing skills with a philanthropic organization. Right now, a high-tech exec's foundation is one of the largest in the United States, with a division on education and world health.

"Through happy coincidence, our families were friends in my hometown of Seattle, and though I'm a little reticent to use my relationship to him, I keep thinking that it would be so much fun to create a position for myself there. And I could be useful to them. For example, I read in the *New York Times* that he was on his way to Bangladesh, where I've spent considerable time. So if we're talking dream job, I would have to say that documenting that foundation's work to see what the organization is really doing for people around the world would be my dream come true.

"Since I'm now thinking out loud here, I have to be honest about my love affair with reporting and being on-air. Producing is fun, but since I've been on the air with CNN on a regular basis . . . I have to say, I love the reporting. And I like the idea of being a woman of a certain age speaking to women over thirty-five who say when they see me, 'Thank God, someone who speaks to me.' I think there is going to be more on that. Then my rational voice interrupts and asks, 'Do you want to be a star? Or do you want to work?' After all, it's hard to be an older woman in a predominantly younger woman's business, especially one where you're photographed every day. It's a cruel business. Your viewers, not to mention the people you work for, often have many more opinions about your hair and voice than about your ability to communicate. And when a network news division downsizes, it is always the senior people with the benefits and larger salaries that are cherry-picked off the payroll to make way for the younger, cheaper talent."

We listened to Robin free-associate about what she wanted to do in her career. Before she started formalizing her lists of her strengths, weaknesses, and transferable skills, we gave her some feedback. First off, it was evident that Robin needed to be in a corporate culture that would allow her to do her thing, reporting and producing, without all the stress of bad office vibes. Since her dream was to work in a nonprofit setting, we also thought she should concentrate on applying her communication skills to charitable organizations, major corporations, and even some Fortune 500 companies with established foundations.

Now that Robin had articulated what she wanted to do when she grew up, we asked her to analyze her professional strengths and document her business skills. So much of her work is about budgets, cutting costs, and managing a diverse group of people, often in crisis situations, yet nothing in Robin's current résumé spoke to those hard-core skills. She had also not analyzed her skills sufficiently. She noted in her résumé her obvious skills as a writer, but neglected to mention her corporate experience as a liaison between the public and large news corporations. She needed to separate or pull apart her skill sets to allow her résumé to give the full breadth of who she was and what she could do. Many employers, for example, wouldn't know that Robin's job of reporting required not just a keen analytical ability and communication skills, but also the ability to write, research, and interview. Robin had developed a nose for the news over the years. She was good at recognizing trends and had perfected the ability to transform her intuitions in a full-blown news story. She could also track a story with the best of them. Often twenty news organizations are going after the same story, and you have to be the one to convey to the people involved that you can tell their story the best. So you need a distinct ability to talk to people, to empathize and be tenacious.

After giving Robin an expanded view of herself, we told her that she was in a perfect position to come up with the "big idea" to enhance the socially conscious or philanthropic image of a big company. Come up with the big idea, we told her, then walk into Michael Eisner's office at Disney (we did suggest she have an appointment first) and say, "I can help Disney be a global healer." If Robin could demonstrate how she could use her background skills to develop and implement new programs that would enhance a corporation's image, she could create her own position within a large company in the process. It's easy when you know how.

Suddenly Robin was excited. Once she knew she could keep her salary high by applying her skills to a large organization, her financial fears were allayed. Her next step, then, was to research companies that might need a senior vice president of corporate communications, and to explore in general the vast terrain of the nonprofit world. We also suggested that Robin look into women-owned production companies, because it's often women who are on the cutting edge of philanthropic pursuits. In terms of Robin's considerable strengths, we told her the best thing about her—besides her experience—was her passion. She carried within her a clear vision of a better world, and she articulated that ideal with clarity and conviction.

Robin was reluctant at first, but we insisted that she not overlook the Internet. With her content background, she was a natural to create a new web site or write for an existing one—perhaps one dealing with health and education. In terms of combining the new technology with her skills and passion, she was suited to doing what is called a Reporter's Notebook, which is a weekly story describing the charitable achievements and gifts of a company's foundation.

Robin's next step was to develop a knockout cover letter including some of the information she had acquired through research. Then it was key that Robin send the letters to specific executives at a high enough level to hire her, whether it was a senior vice president of marketing or divisional president. But no human resource people. No assistants. Since a large company will often underwrite or financially support a community program in order to enhance its image, we suggested Robin contact the people in charge of the corporation's community outreach program. We also suggested she look for familiar names on the company's masthead to see if she could get the inside scoop on the philanthropy programs from members sitting on the board or advisory committee.

Because Robin was torn between her dream career and the realities of life, we thought she should prepare two résumés: one for her on-air background and one for her producing experience. Each résumé would have to show how she could transfer her specific skills into the public relations area or into corporate affairs. Robin's journalism background—her press contacts, research and interviewing skills, her writing and editing abilities—could all segue nicely into a new career opportunity or provide a pit stop before making her career dream come true. Another reason for twin résumés? Because the dual disciplines of producing and reporting often overlapped throughout Robin's career (she was doing on-air assignments during the times she was also a production executive), her résumé did not have a smooth chronology and could seem confusing. Combining her careers on paper could confuse people, but by separating them, she could do a targeted mailing covering both areas of her business background—provided she followed up with a phone call or e-mail to get herself an interview.

Just to play it safe, since creating her own job could take some time, we thought she should not give up on CNN. Robin was, after all, a brand name and extremely well liked. We advised her to take advantage of this popularity by preparing a presentation that would show how she could contribute to the network in a whole new way, either through corporate or documentary work. Robin admitted that during the downsizing she had not spoken up or challenged the corporate decision. We thought it was worth it to try to get together with the powers that be and create a new name for herself as an independent contractor. Psychologically, we also thought that pulling out all the stops and utilizing all of her resources would help purge her of her anger over broken promises.

**Epilogue:** After entertaining a number of career opportunities, Robin decided to become her own boss by forming her own company, West Coast Producers Group, in partnership with her longtime colleague Richard Davies. They had met in 1989 when they both worked for World Vision television, an international relief organization with the primary focus of bringing health care to children of the third world and countries at war. Richard was a producer in charge of fund-raising. Robin was an on-air correspondent on location in West Africa. Since that time, they had worked on a number of projects together, most notably a series pilot called *Jack Hanna's Animal Rescues,* and had continued to produce one-hour television specials for World Vision. As soon as they hung their shingle on the door, the producers of MSNBC's *Headliners and Legends with Matt Lauer* contacted them to produce one-hour biographical documentaries.

We thought opening up her own business was a savvy move, since Robin had an entrepreneurial spirit and desperately needed to get away from the highly competitive corporate culture that defines many of the networks' television news rooms. Now she is completely free and clear to pursue her personal passion, create meaningful content, and, hopefully, one day, through networking and research, to land a production job in the nonprofit world. She is also considering packaging a cable program and including herself as the on-air host. And yes, she has met with that technology mogul, and continues to have an ongoing dialogue with him about where she could go and what she could do for his foundation.

Robin has learned from her career makeover how to think out of the box. She had made the mistake of defining herself and her skills too narrowly and limiting her opportunities. While she feels financially vulnerable about being out there as her own boss, she is now confident she will be able to leverage her skills and use her passion to find work that satisfies her soul . . . the most important requirement of all.

## CAREER-EMERGENCY MARKETING PLAN

There are times when a plan simply to get unstuck won't do. Sometimes the more we need to change our careers the more paralyzed we become. Our emergency marketing plan is designed for those of you who need a housecall from career paramedics. Read on. In just moments good-looking men like

George Clooney from *ER* will be paddling and zapping their way inside your brain to shock you into action, making sure your vital signs (that's your résumé and cover letter) are stable. Put on something white, lie down, and let us rush you to the OR. And besides this marketing plan, don't forget an extra piece of paper so you'll be ready to ask for George's autograph . . . and his telephone number.

## Be Proactive

• Marketing yourself is practically a full-time job. It needs your attention, discipline, and inner strength. Stay focused. You deserve your own attention.

• Harness your energy and systematically follow up all leads. Think outside the box. Pursue contacts and networking opportunities. Approach every prospect as though the contact could lead you to your dream job. You never know who that magic person will be—the one who can hire you, or the one who refers you to your future job simply because they thought you were terrific.

• Be assertive in a friendly way. Don't take no for an answer. Think of ways to overcome any objections you may encounter. Don't take rejection personally. Just think of it as taking you one step closer to your job offer.

## Become Your Own Enterprise

• Know your skills and be able to talk about them easily and intelligently.

89

- Keep in touch with your mentors.
- Interview people who have the sort of job you'd like. What track did they take to get to where they are now? Don't be afraid to ask that friend of a friend. You'd be surprised at how helpful people can be.
- Keep your technical knowledge current.
- Volunteer within your own company for special assignments. Not only will you learn about new areas of the business, you will expand your network of people and build new relationships.
- Cross-pollinate your skills inside your organization by networking among other divisions to create valuable relationships. This will give you additional skills to leverage when you want to make your next career move.
- Join trade and business organizations and have networking lunches or dinners.
- Do your research. Target the companies you'd like to work for.
- R-e-a-d! Trade magazines. Business magazines. *The Wall Street Journal. Forbes. Fortune. Business Week.* Not only will reading keep you current—it will help you stay focused.
- Research. Use the Internet. Log onto corporate web sites and employment web sites such as Monster.com, jobs.com, HotJobs.com, Career.com, Headhunter.net, and Futurestep.com.
- Don't forget to browse on-line. It's amazing the ideas you can come up with in so-called idle moments.

## Target Your Résumés

• Make sure you have more than one résumé, each of which is geared toward a particular area of expertise or interest.

• Refer to the job description you got from your human resources department. Have you incorporated everything from it that you want to emphasize in your résumé?

• Play "Where's Waldo?" Find the executives and department decision makers in the companies for which you'd like to work. Mail *and* e-mail your résumé directly to those persons. E-mail is immediate and implies a sense of urgency. A hard copy can follow in the mail. Follow up with a phone call a few days later.

• Do not send your résumé to the human resources department. Human resource people are not known for being creative. More important, however, they usually don't know what is in an executive's mind. Sometimes, if the right résumé shows up on an executive's desk, he or she may decide to make a replacement. Perhaps someone on staff has been underperforming. Your résumé shows up at the right time and . . . bang! You're hired.

## Try Executive Recruiters

• We've told you never rely on anyone other than yourself, and we mean it. However, that doesn't mean you can't enlist the help of a good executive recruiter.

• Select a handful of established recruiters. *The Directory of Executive Recruiters,* published annually by Kennedy Information, will help you locate those who have expertise in your field.

- Don't spread yourself too thin. Choose two or three recruiters, then interview each one thoroughly.

- All search firms have areas of expertise—whether in finance, legal, entertainment, high-tech, manufacturing, or another area—and clients who keep them on retainer. Find the ones that deal with your targeted companies.

- The recruiter's job is to find a candidate with specific skills to fill a particular position. Your job is to sell yourself to the recruiter so that he or she will want to present you to their client.

- Forge a good relationship with one or two recruiters whom you feel you can relate to and trust. If the meeting doesn't produce results, but the impression you make is positive, you've secured a relationship for the future. A good executive recruiter has the power and ability to help you change your life.

### Cold-Call

- Don't do this on a day that you're feeling less than perfect.

- Call before or after normal business hours and you may be lucky enough to get the hiring executive directly.

- Speak clearly and confidently. Don't hesitate. Remember what you have to offer.

- Befriend assistants. Start chatty conversations that have nothing to do with business—compliment his or her phone style, for example.

- Be respectful of an assistant's time. If the phone is ringing off the hook, postpone the dialogue for another time.

## Keep Records

- Be sure to keep notes and files on every piece of correspondence you send out.
- Organize all of your contacts. Be sure they are in your computer, filed and cross-filed so you can access them easily.
- Keep pertinent information on your networking contacts. It's impressive when you remember a personal story—that tough golf game or the kid's soccer final.
- Note articles about any company you're interested in, and check out what groups or associations its executives belong to.

## Follow Up

- Always follow up with a phone call a week after you've sent a letter.
- Keep up your contacts.
- Request a fifteen-minute meeting. Gaining the opportunity to meet with an executive is of paramount importance.
- If you don't get any results with your top ten wish list of companies, then you must cast a wider net. Sometimes you need to play a numbers game.

# The "Little Black Dress" of Career Makeover Basics

No matter how evolved we become as working women, we still have to go back to basics when we change careers. Pink boas and glitter eye shadow may be all the rage, but we still need that little black dress and strand of pearls. It's the same with careers No matter the depth of our experience and talent, we still need the updated version of career basics: a résumé that shows off our skills, a creative cover letter, and some interview techniques tucked into our tote bag to help answer the occasional tricky question. A witty idea for a follow-up is as essential as blotting your lipstick. And never forget to check out the entire package in a full-length mirror. Your total presentation—on paper and in person—is vital to the process of changing careers.

## RÉSUMÉ

Remember. A career makeover doesn't require a new you. Just a new spin on you—an updated expression of everything you are and can be. Your résumé and cover letter should reflect who you are today, not who you were yesterday. You're not twenty-one and at the starting gate. You're older now and have accumulated valuable experience. We're going to give you pointers on how to package that experience, on how to let your positive attitude shine through—in your résumé, cover letters, and approach to interviews. Think of us as that perfect personal shopper who knows just how to update your look. We understand the world of changing hemlines, lipstick, and whether pink or orange is the new red. We're going to tell you that stating "computer literate" on your résumé is like wearing blue eyeshadow: obvious and unnecessary. We're also going to tell you how best to realign your attitude. *Attitude,* again? We can't emphasize enough how important attitude is to changing your career. You can put on a dress a hundred years old, but no one cares because you're lit up from the inside. Infusing the career basics with a positive vibe will allow your personality to shine so you can stand out and be noticed for the accomplished woman you are. And you are an accomplished woman, aren't you?

Figuring out what goes on your résumé is a little like deciding what you're going to wear on a first date. Are you overly made up? Is your perfume strong or subtle? Do you convey warmth? Passion? Are you clear about what you want in a partner, or are you just fishing? Know what you want and make a good first impression. Your résumé should telegraph the highlights of your career so that a future employer can immediately decide whether he's going to see you or not. A well-written cover letter should make a strong enough impression to get you the attention of the person who's hiring and, with any luck, an interview.

Make sure you dust off and polish up your résumé every six months or so, maybe even replace it altogether. Whether you change careers or not, updating your résumé regularly is invigorating, like a good spring cleaning. The process allows you to think about your accomplishments and, perhaps more important, to document them, to see what you've done and what areas you'd like to develop. And whatever you do, remember to keep your résumé focused. You may feel uncomfortable omitting some of your achievements, but your résumé must telegraph the highlights of your career. It must show that you can match your experience to an employer's needs.

The layout and content of your résumé indicates how well you communicate. It's worth investing some time experimenting with the organization of your résumé, to see which format best suits your experience and ambitions.

## Chronological

By far the most popular format, the chronological résumé allows you to detail your experience in sequence—your last position goes first. This format is especially good if you're not changing industries and the position for which you are applying requires skills similar to those in your last job. A chronological résumé makes it easy for the recruiter to evaluate your experience, but if you are applying for a job in a new industry—if you're going for a radical career makeover—it's up to you to present your experience in such a way that your potential employer can appreciate your value. The temptation with a chronological résumé is to just list your experience. Never forget that your résumé is a powerfully persuasive document. And never forget that it has a twofold purpose: to show what you've done, and to show what you can do.

The chronological format may be tough for someone who hasn't worked in a while or who has moved around a lot—although in today's market "job-hopping" may be considered a plus. If you're uncomfortable with gaps in your history, think about filling them with details of your volunteer work or your other endeavors. (You didn't really spend all that time watching *Days of Our Lives,* did you?)

## Functional

This type of approach allows you to sell your skill sets first and how they apply to the company in which you are interested. A functional résumé is your best bet if you've had multiple jobs and have zigzagged throughout your career without a straight climb up the corporate ladder.

Highlight your skills and accomplishments with a Summary of Qualifications. Use action words like *designed, launched, developed,* and *generated*—verbs that will project your abilities and highlight your responsibilities. Keep it short. Give it punch. You can add your key strengths here if you like and detail the salient points of the business areas in which you were involved. That way anyone scanning your résumé will see at a glance what you've accomplished.

## Sample: Summary of Qualifications

Energetic leader with demonstrated ability to build and manage teams of people in the entertainment industry. Designed and developed business solutions for home video division. Conceptual thinker with capability to build and launch ideas into revenue-generating profit centers focused on global distribution of product. Key strengths are in finance, marketing, and strategic planning.

Below the Summary of Qualifications should be the heading Professional Experience. Here you can generalize in terms of industries. For example, if you've spent ten years in the garment center selling, but have been employed by different companies, you can present it like this:

## Professional Experience

Ten years of high-profile experience in the garment manufacturing business as a sales manager. Hired and managed a large sales force, both domestic and global. Prior to that, spent seven years as an administrator in a health-care organization, responsible for office management and operations.

You also have the option of breaking this down into a list and using bullet points. The emphasis here should be on skill sets, not on years of experience at the same company. This is the way to avoid being categorized as a job hopper—although, in today's marketplace, switching jobs every year or two is not considered a serious flaw.

At the very end of your summary you should supply your work history. Briefly list your experience in chronological order (last position first), including dates of employment, your employer's name, and your title(s). Keep this short, simple, and to the point. The idea here is for your skill sets to get the attention, not the amount of time you've spent at each company. Hopefully, by the time the reader gets to your dates, you will have impressed her with your skills and experience, so she won't be too bothered if you have held numerous jobs or do not have the *exact* background she is looking for.

Don't forget to include any additional experience you think is pertinent to the particular job for which you are applying. If any of your volunteer activities have a specific application that would not only add sizzle but show that you are civic-minded and charitable, include them. Then, at the end of your résumé, comes your education, organizations you are active in, and any publications you may have written or honors received. Remember to keep it brief.

## Résumé Writing Tips

No life stories please. One page, two if absolutely necessary. Be concise. Be convincing. Now's the time to sound like Wonder Woman, full of action. Use words like *engineered, supervised, created, demonstrated, trained, improved, increased,* and *developed.* Be specific with your achievements. By how much did you cut costs to improve the bottom line? Exactly how much money did you raise? How many people did you supervise? What new business units did you help develop?

What merger or acquisition did you participate in and how? If you need help getting in the mood, by all means try on Lynda Carters's garter belt and tiara. Just don't stand by the window.

We like Lynda Lytle's advice to list your skill sets and bullet them. Even if you don't use bullet points in your completed résumé, beginning the process with bullet points will help you to define all your responsibilities, to see just what you achieved in your job, just what the job entails. As Lynda says, "Detail your skills as if they could be applicable to other jobs, because they can. You can be specific without being job specific. That is, show your skills as transferable to other positions."

Customize your résumé as you would your bedroom closet. Separate your skill sets the way you'd separate your clothes—evening gowns here, blue jeans there—so that certain skills and accomplishments can be recognized and appreciated in context. Suit your skills to the occasion or job, so that not only will your prospective employer see what you have to offer, but he will understand immediately that you have what he's looking for. It's a matter of letting the other person know that your accomplishments complement their requirements.

As we've mentioned before, you may want to prepare more than one résumé. Susan Gordon advises, "Feel free to have multiple résumés to emphasize different skills depending on your target market. It's not one size fits all." And be ruthless with your résumé. You don't need to list every job or skill. Again, Gordon says, "I never even use my first two jobs out of college on my résumé. It never occurs to me to reach that far back. Recognize that all of life's experiences are valuable. Evaluate all of your achievements in a new light, but don't feel that you have to list them all on your résumé." A recruiter needs to understand who you are and what you've done. He doesn't need to know where you were during the Vietnam War. Richard Holt, who is with the outplacement firm Lee Hecht Harrison, says that if you're changing careers midstream, your résumé should be an inventory of who you are . . . but hold the twenty-year laundry list. Everything you've done in the past isn't necessarily relevant to what you want to do in the future. Save the references and hobbies for later. No one cares if an over thirty-five-year-old woman likes to water-ski on her time off. And in the category of sad but true, no one cares but you and your husband what you've named your children—and why.

## Debbie Thayer

Reworking your résumé can go a long way to expanding the possibilities of your job search, as Debbie Thayer is learning. When we first met Debbie, she had just recently left Nissan North America after twelve years. She had spent that time in various marketing areas, including advertising, corporate promotions, and sports, entertainment, and event marketing. Her last position was manager of special event marketing. Debbie was a member of the advertising team that launched Infiniti in the United States. She has been responsible for strategic marketing and the management of major multimillion-dollar events and sports sponsorships for Infiniti and Nissan. And prior to that, she managed the marketing and implementation of all programs involved with Nissan's sponsorship of the 1996 Summer Olympic Games in Atlanta.

One of her favorite projects was a program she initiated and developed with the National Geographic Society and the Smithsonian Institution called Earth 2 U, Exploring Geography—a five-year traveling exhibit on world geography. "Earth 2 U was a wonderful way to get Nissan involved in the local markets across the country where they do business, and to be seen as good corporate citizens doing something positive for children and their education."

To further enhance the Earth 2 U program and to make it more newsworthy, Debbie hired Dan Jansen, the Olympic gold medalist in speed skating, to be the program's ambassador and spokesperson. "I wanted someone who could be a role model to the children coming to see the exhibit. An Olympian who had traveled the world for his sport was the ideal solution. The National Geographic and the Smithsonian agreed. In fact, when I presented the idea at the Smithsonian, it got a standing ovation.

"I urged Nissan to take a proactive role with this program, doing more than just paying the sponsorship fee. They agreed with me, and Nissan became a true partner in every sense of the word. We developed a CD-ROM, which we launched at FAO Schwarz in New York, as well as a web site and educational tools for the schools. The kids had so much fun with Earth 2 U they didn't even realize how much they were learning about world geography. I truly believe we helped to broaden the education of countless numbers of children, as well as enhanced Nissan's brand image in the marketplace. It's a wonderful program, and I'm incredibly proud to have been an integral part of it."

Did the program benefit Nissan? You be the judge. Not only did the local Nissan dealers embrace the program and get involved, but Nissan won the first ever Corporate Leadership Award presented by the Smithsonian. Says Debbie, "I was in a room with the senators, Nissan executives, and Smithsonian VIPs when the president of our company credited me with bringing Earth 2 U to life and making it successful. It was truly a proud moment for me."

There is no question that Debbie has a knack for creating corporate programs that fill a particular need. Early in her career at Infiniti, she realized the importance of car sales to women. "Women hate the car-buying process. For that matter, so do men, but they consider it a challenge. Women put it off as long as possible, then drag the nearest guy into the showroom with them, because they know they will not be taken seriously otherwise. That's not right, and I wanted to show women that the Infiniti dealership experience was different. I created the Infiniti Women's Forum. We invited professional and executive women into the showrooms to hear a speaker talk on a subject relevant to their lives. Their desire to hear the speaker was greater than their fear of coming to a dealership. Once they were there, they realized everything was different—the way the showroom looked, the vehicles, and most of all, the way they were treated. By the end of the evening the women were opening car doors, setting up guest drives, and vowing to come back to buy an Infiniti." The Women's Forum was an incredibly successful program that ran for six years at Infiniti and dramatically increased the sales of Infiniti vehicles to women who attended the forum events.

Debbie also spearheaded Nissan's involvement in the 1996 Olympic Games in Atlanta. "It was a very proud time for Nissan, to be involved in such a monumental event as the Olympics. Everyone was involved . . . our dealers, the regional offices, the corporate office, and our manufacturing plant in Smyrna, Tennessee. I coordinated and managed everyone to create an integrated plan going into Atlanta, and on-site at the games. Without a doubt, it was one of the biggest under-takings I've ever been involved in."

So where does Debbie go from here? She tells us her ideal job would be to find a position that would utilize all of her core skill sets and strategic-marketing experience, as well as the experience she has amassed in promotions and event mar-keting. "Marketing has changed dramatically in recent years. Media is so fragmented now, and clients have lots of choices for where to put their marketing dollars. According to *Adweek,* seventy percent of clients' marketing budgets are going to non–media-based efforts, such as promotions, events, and public relations. I want to take advantage of my experience in those areas and integrate it with traditional advertising to give clients what they need today to be competitive. The world is changing so fast . . . twelve years ago when I went to Infiniti, nobody had even heard of the Internet."

While Debbie's diverse background seems ideal for today's marketplace, no one knows quite where to position her. A kind of square peg in a round hole problem, to be sure. As she says, "Most of my peers have a more traditional adver-tising background and go from agency to agency or client to client. I'm not just a 'car guy,' and I bring a lot to the table. I want to broaden and leverage my experience in a senior marketing position either at an agency or client company."

In order to help Debbie get her dream job, we gave her our Unzip Yourself Test. She scored forty-eight, which on our scale means she is quite ambitious, but still aware of the need for balance and moderation. She agrees. She has also received outplacement guidance with Lee Hecht Harrison. Debbie tells us she would ideally like to stay in Los Angeles; however, if the right position became available in New York, she would move to be closer to her elderly parents. A bicoastal position would be ideal. "I used to travel to the East Coast a lot, and it was the best of both worlds for me.

"This has been a wonderful time of transition for me. Friends tell me I look better and happier than I have in years. While I miss the day-to-day activity of business, I feel this transition has been time well spent. I have a solid base of work experience, and I know I have a lot to offer. I come from a typical New England family where my dad always assumed I'd be an English teacher. Considering that, I guess I've come a long way and made my mark on corporate America. I've always known I wanted to do something in the communications and marketing field. That hasn't changed.

"I believe I have one more corporate job left in me when I want to hang up my corporate suits and pumps and go out on the town. My first love has always been writing. I've written a children's book and, like everyone else in LA, a screenplay. Someday I hope to make a living doing what I love best. In the meantime, I would love to find the right position to fit all the pieces of my marketing background into a coherent whole—where I could take a piece of clay and mold my professional life into something new, challenging, and different. I'm an idea person . . . that's my strength. Unfortunately, my weakness is patience . . . not with others as much as with myself."

We urged Debbie to create not only a chronological résumé, but a functional résumé as well. Debbie needed to extract all of her marketing skills and present them up front in a way that can apply to a variety of corporate marketing situations. Due to her twelve years at a car company, her chronological résumé screams "car guy." Also, hiring managers tend to focus immediately on her last position in special-event marketing. The functional résumé, on the other hand, eliminates that focus and allows the reader to pay more attention to her varied skills and experience. The focus should be on her twelve years of comprehensive marketing experience with a major client and on her ad-agency-account management prior to that.

Here are Debbie's two résumés, one chronological and one functional. Both contain the same information, more or less, but notice how the functional résumé spotlights Debbie's skills and accomplishments. The functional résumé prompts the interviewer to be more open in evaluating Debbie's skills, and allows him to focus on her accomplishments within a broader context, not just within the confines of her previous positions.

*Chronological Résumé*

Deborah A. Thayer
Street address, city and state
Phone number
e-mail address

## SUMMARY

Extensive marketing management experience, both at the corporate and agency levels. Proven track record in developing and managing integrated marketing programs, such as the launch of Infiniti, a new luxury automotive brand; the 1996 Summer Olympics; Earth 2 U, a collaborative program with the Smithsonian and the National Geographic; and the US Open tennis tournament. Guest speaker at advertising and marketing functions, and appeared on the Oprah Winfrey Show as an expert on women and cars.

## BUSINESS EXPERIENCE

**Nissan North America, Los Angeles, CA**       1988–2000
**Manager, Special Event Marketing—1998–2000**
Directed marketing strategies and on-site implementation of major Infiniti sports sponsorship and Infiniti dealer announcement shows.

- Directed agency/vendors on all aspects of the US Open, i.e., tickets, credentials, hospitality, vehicle displays, internal communications and dealer incentive fulfillment, which resulted in enhanced brand exposure and good will.

- Managed multi-million dollar Infiniti dealer announcement shows for new product introductions, which created excitement and renewed commitment to the Infiniti brand.
- Oversaw Infiniti dealer incentive program, designed to increase Infiniti sales and awareness.

**Manager, Sales Promotion and Olympic Marketing— 1994–1998**
Developed and executed marketing strategies for a variety of Nissan/Infiniti promotional programs, including the following:

- *1996 Summer Olympic Games*—Directed marketing strategies and programs for Nissan's involvement in the Olympics. Oversaw several tactical teams and the integration of all activities, leading up to the Games, and on-site at the Nissan Pavilion in Atlanta.
- *Earth 2 U, Exploring Geography*—Initiated and developed a relationship between Nissan, the Smithsonian and the National Geographic Society. Managed the development and marketing of ancillary programs for schools, a CD-ROM and a web site. Nissan benefited from increased awareness in the marketplace and dollars from CD-ROM sales. Chosen by Compaq to be part of their educational software package. Won the first ever "Corporate Leadership Award" from the Smithsonian.
- *Infiniti Women's Forum*—Created the Forum to get qualified women into Infiniti dealerships. The program ran for six years and resulted in a measurable increase in female buyers.

- *Infiniti Owner Events*—Managed launch events for introduction of the 1997 Q45 and QX4. Developed unique lifestyle events in seven markets, partnering with American Airlines and benefiting local Ronald McDonald House in each market.
- *Entertainment*—Oversaw product placement in television and film for Nissan/Infiniti. Negotiated a multimillion dollar promotional partnership with Twentieth Century Fox for a 1998 summer release.
  Managed underwriting of Nissan Presents: A Celebration of America's Music. Program hosted by Bill Cosby and aired on ABC.

**Manager, Media Planning—1992–1994**
Responsible for planning/negotiating of Nissan and Infiniti media budgets ($500 million +).
- Successfully leveraged media dollars by strategizing and negotiating value added programs with Condé Nast, Hearst, and Time Warner publishing companies.

**Infiniti Creative/Media Manager—1990–1992**
Managed strategic planning and creative positioning of Infiniti advertising.
- Directed the agency on all advertising issues that impacted brand positioning.
- Negotiated a direct mail campaign targeted to women to launch the new J30.
- Created a series of magazine columns focused on Infiniti vehicles, services and programs, as a result of a value added negotiation.

**Infiniti Advertising Programs Manager—1988–1990**
Directed strategic planning and creative positioning of the advertising campaign that introduced Infiniti—the luxury division of Nissan.

- Member of the marketing team that launched Infiniti in the United States.
- Infiniti had an 89 percent awareness level among consumers within six months.

## OTHER EXPERIENCE

**Campbell-Ewald Company, Los Angeles, CA**—Account Supervisor on Bridgestone Tires
**Needham, Harper & Steers, Washington, D.C.**—Account Executive on: McDonald's (regional owner/operators association), Koni America, WRQX Radio and the National Automobile Dealers Association.

## EDUCATION
**University of Vermont—Mass Communications Major**

## AFFILIATIONS/ACTIVITIES
Board of Directors—Advertising Club of Los Angeles
(4 years)
Board of Trustees—Ronald McDonald House of Los Angeles
Guest Speaker: Evolution of Car Ads Targeted to Women
Guest speaker at Kid Power "98 Marketing Conference"
(on Earth 2 U program)

*Functional Résumé*

### Deborah A. Thayer
**Street address, city and state
Phone number(s)
e-mail address**

**Objective:**   Senior Marketing Director

**Summary:**   Extensive advertising and marketing management experience, both at the corporate and agency levels. Proven track record in developing and managing integrated marketing programs, such as the launch of Infiniti, a new luxury automotive brand; the 1996 Summer Olympics; Earth 2 U, a collaborative program with the Smithsonian and the National Geographic; and the US Open tennis tournament. Guest speaker at advertising and marketing functions, and appeared on the Oprah Winfrey Show as an expert on women and cars.

**Business Accomplishments:**

**Advertising:** Brand Development, Strategic Planning, Media Management, and Brand Enhancement.

- Directed strategic planning and creative positioning of the advertising campaign that introduced Infiniti, the luxury division of Nissan.
- Member of the marketing team that launched Infiniti in the United States.
- Directed the agency on all advertising issues that impacted brand positioning.

111

- Responsible for planning/negotiating of Nissan and Infiniti media budgets ($500 million +).
- Successfully leveraged media dollars by strategizing and negotiating value added programs with Condé Nast, Hearst and Time Warner publishing companies.

**Corporate Promotions/Olympic Marketing:** Brand Development and Sponsorship Management

- Developed and executed marketing strategies for Nissan's involvement in the 1996 Summer Olympic Games.
- Directed tactical teams throughout the country, and spearheaded the integration of all activities leading up to the Games, and on-site at the Nissan Pavilion in Atlanta.
- Initiated and developed Earth 2 U, Exploring Geography, a collaborative effort between Nissan, the Smithsonian and the National Geographic Society. Managed the development and marketing of ancillary programs for schools, a CD-ROM and a website. Nissan benefited from increased awareness in the marketplace and dollars from CD-ROM sales. Chosen by Compaq to be part of their educational software package. Won the first ever "Corporate Leadership Award" from the Smithsonian.

**Event Marketing:** Program Development and Management, Brand Enhancement

- Created the Infiniti Women's Forum to bring qualified women into Infiniti dealerships. The program ran for six years and resulted in a measurable increase in female buyers.
- Managed launch events for the introduction of the 1997 Q45 and QX4. Developed unique lifestyle events in seven markets, partnering with American Airlines and benefiting the local Ronald McDonald House in each market.

- Managed multi-million dollar Infiniti dealer announcement shows for new product introductions, which created excitement and renewed commitment to the Infiniti brand.
- Oversaw Infiniti dealer incentive program, designed to increase Infiniti sales and awareness.

**Public Relations:** Managed PR efforts to support and enhance programs

- Worked with internal PR department to gain exposure for Infiniti and the Women's Forum program.
- Managed Edelman Public Relations in support of the Earth 2 U CD-ROM launch in New York and ongoing support
- Managed Golin Harris in support of Nissan's efforts in Atlanta at the 1996 Olympic Games.
- Collaborated Nissan's New York public relations department to support the US Open tennis sponsorship, as well as the Michael Chang Clinic during Arthur Ashe Kids Day.

**Entertainment:** Brand Enhancement

- Oversaw product placement in television and film for Nissan/Infiniti.
- Negotiated a multi-million dollar promotional partnership with Twentieth Century Fox for a 1998 summer release.
- Managed the underwriting of Nissan Presents: A Celebration of America's Music. Program hosted by Bill Cosby and aired on ABC.

**Sports:** Brand Enhancement and Dealer Relations

- Directed agency/vendors on all aspects of the US Open, i.e. tickets, credentials, hospitality, vehicle displays, internal communications and dealer incentive fulfillment.

113

**Business Experience:**

Nissan North America, Los Angeles, CA
| | |
|---|---|
| 1998–2000 | Manager, Special Event Marketing |
| 1994–1998 | Manager, Sales promotion and Olympic Marketing |
| 1992–1994 | Manager, Media Planning |
| 1990–1992 | Infiniti Creative/Media Manager |
| 1988–1990 | Infiniti Advertising Programs Manager |

**Other Business Experience:**

Campbell-Ewald Company, Los Angeles, CA—Account Supervisor
Needham, Harper & Steers, Washington, D.C.—Account Executive

**Education:**

University of Vermont—Mass Communications

**Affiliations/Activities:**

Board of Directors—Advertising Club of Los Angeles (4 years)
Board of Trustees—Ronald McDonald House of Los Angeles
Guest Speaker: Evolution of Car Ads Targeted to Women
Guest speaker at Kid Power "98 Marketing Conference" (on Earth 2 U program)


Debbie is still searching for her dream job (you'll have to buy the sequel to find out how she's fared), but already she has noticed a big difference in how she's received. Her functional résumé has opened doors for her that, previously, remained shut. No longer the "car guy," Debbie is looking at a wide variety of positions, including leveraging her skills toward an Internet position. Stayed tuned.

## COVER LETTERS

Don't even think about sending a résumé without a cover letter. A résumé on its own can be insufficient, just a compilation of dates and bullet points. A cover letter is your signature, an encapsulation of your personality and accomplishments, your passions and talents, an early indication of your writing skills. Make sure your cover letter creates a great first impression. Make it compelling, but keep it brief. That's the challenge. Here are some tips:

• Use the cover letter to introduce yourself and to state specifically why you want the job they're offering, or why you are interested in their organization. Don't repeat information already included in the résumé. Describe what you can do for your prospective employer and why the two of you are a perfect fit. Let them know they need you.

• If there is no specific job opening, let your cover letter express your general interests in the corporation and their businesses. Declare your strengths. And once again, let them know they need you.

• Name names. If you have been referred by someone the recruiter knows, or if you know someone in common with the interviewer, let her know. It's that six-degrees-of-separation thing.

• Your prospective employer will want to know how your talents and experience will benefit the company. Specifically. And if you've researched the company (and you have, haven't you?), you'll be able to tell how your skills and experience dovetail perfectly with the company's needs.

- Use a little sass and style. It is possible to show charm and wit without acting like a high-maintenance, I-need-time-off-to-do-my-roots type of woman. (Not that we know anyone like that.)

- Get the contact's name and title right. And don't, for heaven's sake, make any spelling mistakes!

- Make the employer's life easy. Be sure your contact information, including your e-mail address, is clearly visible. Let her know—politely, of course—that you'll follow up if you don't hear from her. All's fair in love and job-hunting. If they see you as the tenacious type, you'll get to the top of the paper pile faster. Make sure you've included all of your pertinent information, and then follow up to secure an interview.

- Save any talk about personal or spiritual fulfillment for your book group.

## INTERVIEWS

There is something you should know about interviewers. You stand a good chance of being interviewed by someone young enough to be your daughter. Get used to it. Don't tell her you have a child at home her age or offer to do her laundry if she's pressed for time. Don't ask her whom she's seeing, if he has a job, and if she's eating. At the end of the interview resist all temptation to tell her to call you when she gets home to let you know she's safe. Use your age and experience to your advantage, but don't forget to brush up on new trends in your field and prove you're not inflexible or outdated. This is where attitude really comes into play.

116

The interview process is complex, so prepare yourself. Forget circling the job in the paper, making a date, and knocking on the door. Now you might go through an executive search firm, put your résumé on the Internet, or network your way to an interview. It's a brand-new world out there, and the interview process is lined with hurdles. Here's some help.

The company liked your résumé and cover letter, or you wouldn't be sitting in the room. So go ahead and establish rapport, let the interviewer know that not only do your skills complement her needs, but that you'd be easy and fun to have in the office. Most people, no matter who they are or where they are, think that life is too short to spend time with people who have no sense of humor or personality. So let it rip—appropriately, of course. But first, do your research on the company. Be sure that you are prepared with your own list of questions for the interviewer, whether the interviewer is a human resource person or a decision maker. If you're first interview is with human resources, you need to really impress them with your personality and your background in order to reach the next step in the process. Always give your all, and be the best you can be that day. *And if you are not feeling up to par, reschedule the meeting.* Talk to the interviewer about your skill sets and experience, and be clear about why you think that they could apply in this job with this company. Let him or her know about your industry contacts and why you feel you'd be an asset to this company and that by hiring you they get added value—meaning, you will bring more to the company than just what they may technically require for this specific job.

A few final words? Remember to be cordial to all the receptionists and secretaries. You'll score big points for that.

And go ahead and notice any family photos and comment on them. It's a great icebreaker!

## Information Interview

Interviews take practice. The more you do them, the better you become. The information interview can be a great learning experience and a great confidence builder too. Notice how your interviewer checks you out from head to toe—and we mean head to toe—the moment you walk in the room. So always wear amazing shoes that reflect the corporate culture. You think we're kidding? Birkenstocks for an Internet start-up. Pumps for the corporate world. Knowing what to wear will give you confidence. Be poised. Approach every information interview as though you're Lana Turner at Schwab's. She didn't go there dressed to the nines and sip sodas for nothing. She went there to be discovered. And that's how you need to approach every information interview. As if you're going to be discovered.

**HOT TIP:** The information interview is like a blind date. You're not officially going out; you're just looking each other over to see if you're interested.

Sue Tucker, a career management consultant from Lee Hecht Harrison, says, "Sometimes in an information interview you meet with someone so sharp you say to yourself . . . *I've just got to find a place for them.* I always tell my clients to treat an information interview as a networking meeting. And you better have your presentation rock solid."

Here are some typical interview questions, courtesy of Pamela:

- What are your strengths and weaknesses?
- What have been your two greatest accomplishments?
- Describe a difficult situation and how you dealt with it.
- What do you think people say about you?
- What aspect of your work do you love or hate the most?
- Where do you want to be five years from now?
- Why are you leaving your current job?
- Tell me about yourself. (Some executives love this broad question, so don't be caught off guard, organize your thoughts and be prepared.)

"Since so much of today's interviewing is behavioral," says Sue Tucker, "you have to hope for good chemistry as well as a skills match. Employers are not only looking for skill sets and competency. They are looking for a fit. A total package. They look at the résumé and ask you about your experience. But most of the time is devoted to seeing how well you'd fit into the company."

## Breaking Bread

A dinner or lunch interview is generally a more relaxed way to get together with your interviewer. If the occasion is a meal rather than an office visit, you can bet that your interviewer is trying to find out how you'll fit in with his team and corporate culture. Rita Sue Siegel, an executive recruiter, likes taking her candidates to dinner because she feels people are more relaxed, more likely to show who they really are. Make sure there's nothing about you that screams *weird*. Be polite. Don't drink. And don't eat anything green that will stick in your teeth, or large enough to require the Heimlich maneuver.

## Committee Interview

An interview committee is made up of a group of people who each represent a different department within the company. Since this approach is collective, you can bet that you will be evaluated from varying angles—great for a woman who has had a wealth of experience and who knows how to transfer her skills. The committee will want to see how you fit into the organization as a whole, so it may come up with a problem-solving task to determine your potential for meeting multiple needs within the company. If you know ahead of time that you're going into a committee interview, ask the person arranging the meeting for the names of those attending. Find out the job titles and responsibilities of each person, and use your research skills to do some fast digging to determine their roles within the company. Know beforehand if there's a particular ongoing project in which your expertise may be helpful. Keep your eyes and ears open.

HOT TIP: "Start off selling them on you, but midway through mention how this is a big decision for you too and turn the tables so they start selling you back."—*Cynthia Cleveland.*

The interview process often intimidates women. As Sue Tucker says, "Many women come in and don't understand the extent of what they have to offer. They don't realize the value of their professional past, and worst of all, they're often under the old misconception that they shouldn't brag. Women need to learn how to toot their own horns. They need to know how to talk about their own contributions." She advises building self-esteem by rehearsing what you're proud of. Be clear about your accomplishments so you won't be beaten down by an interviewer."

Rehearse the interview dialogue. Prepare notes. Go to the company's web site. Anticipate their every concern. If there's a point on your résumé that's weak, if you've been fired or downsized, be honest. Be factual. Everyone's had ups and downs.

Try to speak about your past comfortably, without rancor or bitterness. If you weave your personal life into your professional stories, you will seem accessible and self-confident. Always accentuate the positive.

Applicants are always asked at the end of the interview whether they have questions about the company or the job. Never ask about the compensation package. Instead use this opportunity to demonstrate your passion as well as to clarify anything you may not understand. It makes you look very smart and as if you are engaged in a process, not manipulating a one-sided power play.

Try to find something in common with the young man or woman who will be interviewing you—even if their arrogance makes you want to inflict bodily injury. You need to know that the Backstreet Boys are not a gang, and that Britney Spears is not a form of asparagus. Take a Berlitz course on generation X and Y. Trust us, it's a whole new language.

Take heart: There are some recruiters on your side. Eunice Azzani, a recruiter for Korn/Ferry International thinks so highly of the interview process (more so than of the résumé and cover letter), that she uses it almost exclusively for hiring her company's employees. "Paper doesn't tell me anything. I want to find out who people are. I want to understand where their talents can go, and I usually can't find that out on paper. I use the interview process to try and uncover candidates. I want to know them, although sometimes it's very hard. I have had experiences when a candidate is in my office and she's extraordinarily polished. She's giving me articulate answers and saying all the right things . . . and I have no idea who she is. It becomes a challenge to really get people to reveal themselves. I look for the gleam in someone's eyes. I can shop résumés. But I'm looking to match opportunities with my client's higher skill sets, their communication skills, their leadership, their resilience."

## So You're Over Thirty-Five

You can't grab the latest fad off the rack when you're over thirty-five, and you can't play the job market as if you were twenty. No doubt about it, a longer résumé requires a different tack. We got the inside scoop on getting hired from top executive recruiters, the experts who place clients in major corporations all day long. Here's a roundup of pointers from some of the top search consultants in the country. No, you don't have to send in a check. Just keep reading.

Neil Lenarsky, an executive agent with Strategic Transitions Inc., says that as soon as he shakes hands with a prospective candidate, he's looking for clues to what captivates, motivates, energizes, and electrifies him or her. "The thing an interviewer will pick up," Neil explains, "is what parts of their career turned them on. Do they remember a Sunday night when they couldn't wait to get to work on Monday morning? I'm looking to unlock that excitement. Maybe they've never had it, or maybe they've got it, but they need to improve where they are."

Rita Sue Siegel takes it further when she says, "The candidate has got to be some kind of special person. She's got to look you right in the eye. And then when you ask her a question, no matter how deep or shallow, she's got to take you very seriously. She really has to want to make you understand what she's about. She really has to show genuine interest in the process. I want to walk in and say to myself, *This is somebody.*"

Lenarsky believes that by the time a woman reaches forty, he can see a diminishing fire, a lack of optimism. He believes that if there's an age bias, it's because younger women tend to demonstrate more enthusiasm. Interestingly enough, it doesn't have anything to do with looks. In a search where he sent out a thirty-three-year-old and a forty-two-year-old for the same job, the older woman was by far more attractive.

But the younger woman had fire in her belly, and that earned her the job.

All of the executive recruiters we spoke to agreed that employers are not looking at age, they're looking at energy and enthusiasm. They're looking at depth and experience—which is in our favor. They're looking for youthful qualities. Your hair can be gray, but you must have an optimistic attitude.

Knowing what you want to do and what kind of culture or work environment you want is crucial. This includes being able to talk about what you want to do down the line. As Richard Holt advises, "Down the line is going to be different for a woman who is forty-five as opposed to thirty-five. Take a long view of what it is that you want to do down the road. And then look at everything you have, your personal assets— your skills, and your abilities. Those are the tools that will get you to that long-range goal."

Neil Lenarsky agrees that focus is a huge component of a successful career transition. "The biggest mistake a woman can make is not defining herself, not doing the right research." As a career coach, he wants to know the professional turn-ons of a candidate. What kind of work has she felt passionate about? To that end he always asks what the five most electrifying moments are of someone's career. "Usually," Neil explains, "it's just one moment, maybe twenty years ago. But I have them go back to that moment. People start a career when they're young, and get told they're good at it. So they get pulled into a lifetime of doing something they're technically and strategically good at, but not passionate about. And then one day they look in the mirror and they say, "What have I been doing all these years?""

Another piece of advice everyone had for us was to think of your skill sets as your marketing tool. Tell people what you have to offer. You can't sell your services unless you articulate where you excel. We know we've told you this before, but for women, tooting our own horn and getting noticed is half the battle. The way things used to work in an interview, where you'd sit in a room and be asked questions, no longer applies. Now you have to do a presentation on why you want the job and how your performance would benefit the company.

You must research the company and research the job. Interviewers want to know what you know about their company. Have you done any homework? Almost all of the information about any public company or well-known organization is available on the Internet. If you go in unprepared, you look lame. So, prepare some thoughtful questions about the company and the job. Try pretending you're playing the corporate version of *The Match Game*. It's important to share with the interviewer how you would fit in, in terms of the philosophy and culture of the company.

Rita Sue Siegel says she doesn't mind if somebody tries to take control of an interview. "If a candidate doesn't think I'm asking the right questions, then I like it when she starts to manipulate the conversation so she can tell me what she wants to tell me. We need to have a person like that."

Further your knowledge of a company or organization. Neil Lenarsky suggests finding someone inside the company to give you the inside scoop.

A high scorer among our tipsters was the recommendation to establish a rapport with the interviewer. Notice what's in the office, on the walls, on the desk, and don't be afraid to show off your observational skills. An interviewer is looking to see if you are very engaged in the process of the interview.

Be prepared to talk about your technological skills. Now that we're older, we have to demonstrate we've figured out how to perform all of our skills on-line, and with the latest equipment. Let them know that you can "drag a mouse" with the best of them. Update yourself. Just as we show you in the Makeover section of the book, a consultation with a hair, makeup, and wardrobe person to update your look is a great investment in yourself. Take a test to see if this advice applies to you. If you wear your hair the same way you did in your high school yearbook photo, you definitely need to listen to us. It's silly, but if you walk into an interview with an old pair of shoes and an old bag, the interviewer may think you are an old bag. Don't even let them go there. Treat yourself to a new look, and walk into a room with confidence, your newly coifed head held high.

Our roundtable sang like a choir over this point: If you're changing careers, EMPHASIZE TRANSFERABLE SKILLS, AND PROVIDE SPECIFIC EXAMPLES. Look for openings that will allow you to talk about your strengths. Make sure you articulate how what you've done in the past transfers to what the employer needs today and in the future.

Richard Holt warns that you can't always rely on the interviewer to get those skills and needs talking to each other. The interviewer isn't always capable of making those connections, so you must connect the dots. Renée Fraser advises to rattle off your core skill sets and to be prepared to do so in the first sixty seconds of an interview. And while you're at it, allow your sense of maturity and perspective to be communicated.

"I know when I hire I look for maturity. Calm and grace under pressure when you are our age are a plus because we know how to rise above petty politics."

Many organizations are looking for team players from different fields. Give credit for your successes to other people with whom you've worked and to other companies that have increased your learning curve. You seem less invested in ego and more interested in teamwork. Don't be afraid to speak your mind. Eunice, who specializes in placing women over thirty-five, has this advice. "I have opinions, and I'm not afraid to put my opinions out there. It's more attitude than skill. I think I'm smart. That's how I present myself, and I feel my opinions and experience are just as valuable as anyone else's at the table."

If you have a sample of your work that you're proud of, bring it along for a "tease." Not a diary, but a graphic or a mission statement or . . . offer up a little taste of your talent. It shows that you already possess the necessary skills, and you're not afraid of putting yourself out there for review.

Don't rag on anyone else you've worked with. It always turns out to be the interviewer's best friend. Haven't you ever heard of karma? Life happens in cycles of reward and punishment. And if you *kvetch* about another person or company, the interviewer will think it's just a matter of time before you start in on him.

And don't forget, your attitude is paramount, your focus on the skills and gifts you can contribute. If you're depressed, angry, or bitter, an employer will smell you a mile away. That's what happened to our third makeover candidate Debra Rosner.

## Debra Rosner—Career Makeover

When we first met Debra Rosner, she had spent ten years in the music business as a public relations and marketing executive, but was looking to make a change. After months of trying, she wasn't able to even get her foot in the door of a recognized company. Having failed to make a career move to a brand-name music agency or studio, she eventually went out on her own.

As Debra described it, she was always the bridesmaid, never the bride. After sending résumés and following through with e-mails and phone calls, invariably the position she applied for went to someone inside the company. Even worse, she would sometimes hear about a position after it was filled. Debra had conducted an extensive job search, using many of the tricks of the trade we address in the book. She reworked her résumé to highlight her skills and had made a number of cold calls, always targeting the person who was hiring. She had also perfected the imaginative, get-yourself-noticed personal marketing tool, and after one particularly promising interview even sent funny toys and messages. Nothing.

On the surface, Debra's challenge seemed to be the eighties metal bands she'd managed and publicized, like *Poison* and *Brittany Fox*. All successful acts, but by her own admission, way out of the mainstream. Debra questioned whether her fringe clients were a turnoff to the more conservative record labels to which she aspired. Nevertheless, we all agreed that she possessed the skills and experience to leverage toward *any* job in the music business.

So, what was the problem? In terms of her presentation, Debra still had an "alternative" look: hair severely pulled back in a ponytail, a too tight T-shirt, and a no-makeup, washed-out complexion. A totally noncorporate look. And what was worse, her discouragement and resentment at not being able to crack a recognized company was apparent. Although open and willing to listen, Debra had a of chip on her shoulder that she was unable to hide.

Throughout her professional life, Debra had been given feedback praising her creativity and her ability to juggle a million tasks at the same time. But she had also been told she was too emotional. Former employers thought Debra had difficulty judging when it was wise to get upset and when to let go of her drama and anger. It was as if every problem that presented itself was of the same magnitude and required the same amount of emotional output. As a result, she spoke too fast and got too excited about little things. When her defense system kicked in to protect her ego, she was then seen as either too harsh or, conversely, as incapable of playing hardball.

We spent time helping Debra revise her résumé. That was easy. We showed her how to tailor it to a potential job, making it more general to emphasize her skill sets, not just her experience in the music industry. That helped Debra get calls from *outside* the music business. A first. We also helped her update her look so that she looked as if she was going to an office, not a rock concert. That gave Debra more confidence. Then we put her in touch with Dr. Lois Frankel, a psychologist and president of the Los Angeles–based Corporate

Coaching International, who talked to her at great length about her work style and needs.

Now, Debra tells us, she feels more comfortable being herself. "In terms of my behavior, I've learned to be much more aware of the impressions I'm making. I tend to be hyper, and now I know I can slow myself down. I can express my creativity and excitement without going over the top. I will never again cover up who I am. I am energetic and creative, but I need to remember that I don't need to bowl people over. I can control it." Debra took that knowledge with her to interviews. "I understood how to take control of the interview. I went in with informed questions and specific facts as to how what I had to offer matched up to their needs. Other career books didn't prepare me mentally, but now I feel comfortable being myself, so I'm much more confident. My inward changes encouraged me to make changes in my behavior, which has been important not only in getting a job, but inside the job—with clients and colleagues. Now I feel more professional."

Debra had always wanted to work for a nonprofit organization, to transfer her skills from the music industry into something more philanthropic. In the past she had always helped major corporations make money, but she didn't feel as if she was contributing. "I wanted to help people through a charity or through health care," she says. "I've always volunteered over the years, hoping I could find a job in this field."

Debra applied to the City of Hope for what she thought would be her ideal job, one that would satisfy her on a soulful and professional level. Unfortunately, after several weeks of meetings, the position was eliminated and absorbed into another department. This time Debra wasn't crushed or resentful. "I retooled my résumé and was offered a job by a music company as an account executive in the sales area, a job with which I had never made it to first base before."

Working in sales for just over a year, Debra increased their business by over eighty percent. But then management decisions were being made that she didn't agree with. "Before my makeover I would have complained and retreated behind a dark cloud or gotten way too emotional because things weren't working out," she says. "This time I went job searching before that critical time and logged onto the Internet. I couldn't believe it. The City of Hope job site showed that job I had originally wanted had been refunded and reposted! I had to call several times but was finally able to arrange an interview for myself. This time, with patience and perseverance, I got my dream job. I am now the marketing relations manager for the City of Hope National Medical Center. Learning how to readjust my attitude and retailor my career basics all worked. I was able to remarket myself into my dream job." We rest our case.

Several career experts spoke to the issue of attitude. Sue Tucker tells of a successful woman she was working with who was transitioning from a bank environment. She had been downsized, and her business unit was let go, along with her entire team. "The minute the bank was sold, her unit sat there for three months, and my client, who loved the action of the job, was bored to tears. We explored other professional avenues, until one day she said she couldn't make use of my services anymore. Why not? Because, she said, 'I have a sports utility and I'm strapping on my surfboard and skis and I'm taking off.'

"Here was a successful woman in her early forties—single, independent, and burned out. She was smart to take off. She returned rested and ready to start looking at her skills, even though she was still in a fog as to what she wanted to do. So here she is, an MBA out of Columbia being courted by the competition for a six-figure salary. But that's not where her passion lay. She's a sky diver. A skier. An outdoors woman. She's a risk taker, and my challenge was to match her skill sets to her passion. To do that we had to prepare two résumés for her. We wrote a really effective résumé that was targeted toward her banking–financial-services background, with a chronological format. That showed who she's worked with, her overall accountability, and her bulleted track record. Then we prepared a second résumé where we targeted her skill sets, and offered a summary statement of her hard skill sets, couched in language acceptable to *Outward Bound*. We avoided the financial lingo and acronyms that would turn off someone outside the world of banking, but we included enough so that a prospective employer could see the tie-ins between her skills, her passions, and the needs of their corporation."

Sometimes when you're in transition, you just need to take a time-out and not move quickly. Change can make you angry or super depressed—not a good frame of mind to be in when looking for other opportunities. As Sue Tucker knows, "It's very challenging when a client needs money right away and doesn't have the luxury of time off. In that case I tell clients to talk to someone about the way they're feeling—a professional or a really close friend whom they respect . . . and then get moving.

"Sometimes, depending on how a woman is feeling—if, say, she's in the advanced stages of burnout—she may very well want to duck into a safe harbor, a mindless job that doesn't require much thought or stress level. That's understandable, but the fear is that while she's working the no-stress job, she's losing time and losing ground, perhaps running the chance that she'll get bored, and that her self-esteem will go in the toilet again."

Sue goes on to say, "The key, if you can, is to take some time out, because for folks who don't, it's like a rebound marriage. There's the divorce, and then two months later they're in love, and three months later they're married, and guess what the fallout rate on rebound marriages is?"

# How to Handle Interviewers

There are several kinds of interviewers, and each has a quirkiness all his or her own. You need to decide what you want to say before you even enter the room, so that no matter what you're asked, you'll be able to convey to the interviewer that you're the right woman for the job.

Here are some tips on how to handle typical interviewer types:

## The Yakker

This is the interviewer who launches right into a dissertation on his trip to Europe or the big fish he caught in Montana. You could be charmed by him if you weren't in the position of having a limited ten minutes to make a lasting impression.

The trick here is to look for segues like the ones Jay Leno uses when he performs his monologues on *The Tonight Show*. Such as, "You just got back from Europe? I understand you've just opened a division in Europe." Keep the interview on track.

## The Hostile Type

This is the guy who will put you on the defensive. You know, the kind of person who appears to be hostile for absolutely no reason, since you just met him, and by the way, didn't he invite you into his office? Still, he will try to make you feel as if somehow you are an imposition and that you are taking up his valuable time (usually spent shooting pencils into a corkboard).

This is the kind of interviewer who makes you wonder what you're doing there in the first place. His lead-off question will be: "So, what makes you think you're qualified for this position?" Don't make the mistake of letting him remind you of every guy you've ever known who mistreated and underestimated you, because then you'll give him exactly the response he's looking for. Align yourself with the enemy, and respond, "I can understand why you would ask me that question . . ." and let him have it.

## The Off Topic Type

Then there is the bungling interviewer, the kind of person who asks you questions that are totally irrelevant both to the job and to you. You don't really care about the movie she saw the night before. And you're not at all interested in the fact that she can't get her message light to stop blinking. Be prepared to talk about yourself with organized thoughts. Carry on as if you're dealing with a rational human being.

### The Distracted Type

You know this type too. The phones are ringing, but he doesn't tell the assistant to hold his calls. He's smoking or eating or fiddling with the toys on his desk. He has all the earmarks of a child with attention deficit disorder who's forgotten to take his Ritalin. He's conducting business while you're sitting there—not only acting unprofessionally, but showing off his power, like a guy talking on a cell phone in a bar just to impress you. Don't throw a drink in his face, instead ask him up front, "Is this not a good time?" This lets him in on the fact that you know he's being rude and also gives him the benefit of the doubt. He may actually be having an unusually busy day. If that's true, then you should indeed come back another time when he's going to be more receptive to hearing you.

## Follow Through

After you've been on your interview date, then you have to decide if you're going to be a "Rules girl" and not call until the company does, or if you're going to do the pursuing. Here are some guidelines:

Don't send flowers and cookies as a follow-up. Do something creative that reflects the corporate culture, or capitalize on something the interviewer shared about himself or the company. Cool but not tacky.

Generally people who are hiring are overworked and over-booked. So asking during of the interview if it's okay to call in a couple of weeks shows you are interested, without making a pest of yourself. This will help you to stand out in her mind when she's making her final selection.

Richard Holt says that, "Once you've made initial contact with somebody, you need to touch base roughly every ten working days, or twice a month. Have a reason to call. *I've made a change on my résumé. I saw an article in the paper about your company.* You could send the article ahead of time, then call to touch base. If you don't have an agenda, then even calling every ten days is kind of annoying."

Get the e-mail address of the person you're connecting with. Use that to make your initial contact. E-mail every ten working days. People respond to their e-mail faster and more frequently than they respond to voice mail or notes. Most executives find it easier to answer an e-mail because they're sitting with their hands on the keyboard and, *hey, . . . there's the message,* front and center. And isn't that really the whole point of the follow-up, to keep you front and center?

Personally, Richard Holt advocates the sticky-note methodology. "There's no science behind this," he says. "But if you see an article in the paper, copy it, cut it out, and write a Post-it that says 'I saw this and thought you may be interested.' Then send it off so that when you next call, you'll have something to talk about. 'Did you get that Post-it I sent you?' Or 'that joke?' Creativity is very important."

And hang in. Sue Tucker explains that the whole trick to surviving the process of changing careers or jobs is perseverance. "A woman I had been seeing called me and said that at the end of her self-discovery process and résumé building, she still didn't know what to do. And I said, 'The problem is you expect a miracle. This is hard work and I don't want to disappoint you. You think perhaps that I'm a genie and that I'm going to give you all the answers.' I had to do the tough-love talk. I'm here to partner with my candidates, but they have to do the footwork."

That means information interviews. Networking. Internet research. Magazines. Sue continues, "Most of my clients are very smart and sophisticated. They know how to perform, and they're paid well for it. Unfortunately, few of them know how to negotiate their way through a transition. In this business, you're holding up the mirror of life and looking at it all the time. It makes you think of your weaknesses. But transitioning careers and jobs means rejection. It brings up fears and anxieties and self-doubt because they're going into a judgmental environment. Yes, someone is going to be judging you sitting across the table. And that's uncomfortable."

# Chapter Five

# Corporate Culture

You wouldn't go on vacation without first researching the country you were planning to visit, would you? So why join a company without firm knowledge of the people who work there, the company customs, and the business prospects? You'd like to know if a political coup and takeover were imminent in that holiday destination, wouldn't you? So why wouldn't you try to find out if your prospective employer is deep in turmoil during an end-of-year rainy season—or drought? Let's face it: if you're going to be held hostage, it may as well be in a place under sunny skies, with a steady stream of tropical drinks with those little umbrellas on top.

Corporate culture is extremely important. It can determine your professional comfort level and affect how well you adjust to your new corporate surroundings—not to mention your success on the job. So before joining any organization make it a point to find out about the culture. How is the company doing? The bottom line can have a huge effect on culture and morale, so listen to what people in the industry have to say about your prospective employer. And what about so-called secondary issues? We all pay attention to title and salary when we're job-hunting, but what about dress code, bureaucracy, benefits (do they have a gym or day care?), and, most important of all, the ratio of men to women. Low representation of women could mean poor possibilities of advancement and promotion. So be warned.

You'll get your first impression of a company's culture the moment you step off the elevator. Notice how the receptionist greets you. Analyze the interior architecture. Is it closed or open space? Are there people in the halls talking and laughing? What about artwork, or the lack of it? Pay attention to the intangibles and trust your instincts.

Amy Ephron has had more than her fair share of battles with corporate culture. This talented screenwriter, producer, and author of six books, most recently the best-seller *White Rose,* made over her own career from studio executive to novelist without any help from us. But not without a struggle. Even though her sister, acclaimed director Nora Ephron, coined the term *baby mogul* for her successful little sister, Amy is not a product of entitlement. Rather, her prolific writing and international speaking engagements are a direct result of pure talent and backbreaking time spent hunched over legal pads and computer screens and trying to avoid looking at early rejection slips from publishers. But we wanted to relate her story to you because she exemplifies the woman who is the proverbial round creative peg in the square corporate hole. And because she describes her escapades in such a funny way, we wanted to scoop her stories before she gets the idea to tell them herself.

In 1975, at an early age, Amy began her career in New York as a book scout for a Los Angeles producer, combing publishing houses in search of hot books that could be adapted for the big screen. After a stint working for Al Pacino and becoming known as a woman who attracted both writers and talent to her projects, she moved up the ladder to an executive position at Columbia Studios in Los Angeles. While living on the East Coast, Amy had managed to avoid a lot of heavy-duty Hollywood politicking. But now as a part of the establishment that drove the business, she was less than thrilled at having to deal with the competitive good old boys with the bad tempers and matching attitudes toward women. "These guys were so nasty," she recalls. "They were thrilled by other people's failures. Nothing made them happier than watching the competition fall to their knees. Not only did this behavior apply to the outside world, I watched as my own colleagues were ostracized for failure. If you were the executive on a picture that opened badly on Friday . . . by Monday morning everybody had stopped talking to you. I remember Albert Brooks opened a film called *Modern Romance* to low box-office ratings and no one ever spoke to him from the studio again. The truth is, in a business that crosses the line between art and commerce, creativity and bottom-line numbers, 'the pressure to succeed' is an oxymoron.

"The head of the studio at the time was a man who walked the halls with a book under his arm called *Fifty-two Plots*— or maybe it was *Twenty-seven . . .* , I can't remember—but he believed the basis of every screenplay was contained in some plot contained in the book underneath his arm. I didn't happen to agree, and so began my problems as a creative executive who was hired to voice opinions that most of the guys running the studio didn't want to hear.

"The hardest thing I noticed early on was that if I made a mistake, they would point a finger at me. But if I was successful, they would take all the credit. The executives were all so concerned with their own success, and I never understood the race. I was naïve . . . still am. I remember when the movie *Tess* came into the studio. It was an engagingly beautiful piece of filmmaking with none of the traditional elements of a commercial blockbuster. The powers that be hated that it was an old-fashioned period movie. No one had ever heard of the star Nastassia Kinski. There was still controversy swilling around the fugitive director Roman Polanski. It was pre arthouse studio release time and even pre female demographic. But as soon as I saw it, I knew this could be a big movie for us, and I campaigned for it like crazy. Finally the boys acquiesced, reasoning that the lone female executive may be right and they threw dollars at the movie for promotion and advertising.

"The rest of course is history. The movie was not only critically acclaimed but made a lot of money for the studio. I had fought the good fight and was naïve enough to think I had won. When the reviews came out, I was shocked to read the studio head's revisionist version of how he had come to make this bold, brave decision to bring *Tess* to the studio. Without even mentioning my name, he told the press that he and his wife had first watched this cinema verité in a screening room together, and when it was over, his wife turned to him and said, 'You have to release this.' It was as if I didn't exist. The whole thing was like a knife in my stomach, and what I learned was that not only did these guys want the competition to fail, they wanted people underneath them to fall off the truck as well. Or at least not be successful enough to steal the thunder from them.

"Occasionally being the only woman was a good thing. I remember sitting in a screening room with the boys watching a movie called *Das Boot*—one of the most memorable films about the horrors of war I'd ever seen. When the lights came on, they all looked at me, thinking a woman would never respond to the material. But in fact I loved it, and as a result of my accolades and assurances that women would go see this film, we distributed it. The director of that film has since gone on to take the helm of several successful American movies, most recently *The Perfect Storm*.

"Then there was the *E.T.* fiasco. We had paid for Steven Spielberg, then fresh from his success with *Close Encounters of the Third Kind,* to hire the acclaimed Melissa Mathison to write his next project. The draft was slipped to me and I flipped. It remains to this day in my opinion one of the best scripts ever written . . . hauntingly simple without hype or guile . . . dialogue perfect . . . a blueprint ready for Steven to shoot. But somehow they felt that *E.T.* was a children's film—long before children's films were considered to be the moneymakers they are today. And we already had the extra-terrestrially themed *Starman* in development. And if we could only make one of them, the head marketing guy—and the studio head's right-hand man—argued he had completed a survey that proved *Starman* would be the greater hit. I ranted. I raved. I lost. And that is how Columbia Studios came to put *E.T.,* one of the most successful movies of all time, into turnaround . . . and how Universal Studios made one hundred and seventy million dollars without once calling home.

"One of my professional mandates was to discover and sign talent before the rest of the world even knew they existed. Since I had a lot of friends over at *Saturday Night Live* and it was such a hotbed for budding comedians, I was exposed at an early stage to the talent of a man by the name of Eddie Murphy. At the time, I sensed he could have an extraordinary range on film, similar to Richard Pryor. I had already developed *Stir Crazy,* one of the first films to top the one-hundred-million-dollar mark in sales, and I intuitively knew Eddie Murphy could be the next guy to send us laughing all the way to the bank. So three weeks after *E.T.* had left the building, I signed Eddie Murphy to the studio for a mere fifty thousand dollars . . . a very lowball deal for Hollywood. I put together a little reel of Eddie's work, gave it to the studio head, and went home with the flu. I had not even reached my home when my cell phone rang with news that not only had Eddie Murphy's contract been canceled, I had been fired."

In hindsight the Eddie Murphy debacle was just the straw that broke the camel's back. The same studio head who had claimed credit for *Tess* and had disregarded Amy's opinion on *E.T.* had also hired another woman, who, unlike Amy, respectfully knew her place in the studio system—and in the early eighties there was only room for one woman. But what may have brought down the ax on Amy's corporate career was the fact that some of the Hollywood heavyweights, knowing of Amy's affinity for creative, money-making material, often called her . . . and not necessarily the studio head. In our opinion that sounded her death knell right there. You are, after all, known by who's on your speed dial, and when those people are calling your underling . . . Houston, we have a problem. However, she says, "I will always be proud of the fact that with my last gasp of breath at the studio I put *Out of Africa* into development—ironically one of the biggest coups of my career.

"This was also a time when the business of moviemaking was changing. With all the corporate upsizing, the business became far more about Coca-Cola and stock options and less about what script would make a good movie. A lot of the good old boys in those days became very rich, and with the film business more concerned with the bottom line than the story line, the great days of filmmaking gave way to the independent film movement. The business had suffered two devastating blows that year, a writers strike and an actors strike, and I felt divided loyalties. On the one hand my job was to yell at writers and convince them to keep working on their scripts. But on the other hand, I come from a family of writers whose parents were instrumental in setting up the Writers Guild, and I couldn't bring myself to go against them in principle or in action.

"The fact is," says Amy, "I never fully understood and absorbed that corporate America is about making money. I can read a movie contract and I know exactly what it means. But I was old-fashioned in the sense that my strength was that I could hear a story and know whether it would work up on the screen . . . and how to cast it. So when the ax fell and I was immediately offered another studio job, I turned it down. Deep down I felt that I belonged to the other side and always had. At heart I knew I was a writer . . . felt more comfortable as a writer, and even though my first novel was rejected by thirteen publishers, it did eventually see the light of day as a mass-market paperback and went on to become a best seller with rave reviews. So my decision was validated.

"What I don't miss about the culture is that 'pit in my stomach feeling' reminding me that today might be the day I'll be fired. It's such a revolving door, and the film business is the only business that when a new regime comes in, they throw out all the inventory and all the people responsible for it. I just couldn't live that way anymore. I also felt that I kept my professional relationships to men at bay. I stayed guarded and emotionally distanced because I never wanted people to think that the reason I was successful in this business was because I had slept my way there.

"After much struggle I have experienced success as a novelist and a screenwriter. In terms of being outside the eye of the corporate hurricane, I'm happy at home because it's obviously easier to have my own schedule with my three kids. But if I'm on deadline or in the middle of an artistic meltdown, then I'm not sure my being home is good for them. I do miss all the activity, the action, the constant ringing of phones, with the people always wanting something from me. Although there are times at home, between work and the kids, my house is as chaotic as an office. What I miss most of all is the feeling that you get when you discover a new talent or read an incredible first draft of a screenplay, that feeling of your bat connecting to the ball and knowing that eventually that ball will become a home run. So I would have to say I would never say no to another stint in corporate America. But I would certainly make sure I was in a situation where my contributions were appreciated, where I nurtured the people who worked for me and I was nurtured by the people I worked for. That's a feminine approach to business and the only one I could live with."

Pamela, who has made it her business to keenly observe corporate culture, had an unforgettable experience in the early seventies. She was a young woman who had recently started in the executive search business when Avon had called to ask her to a meeting. This was in the days of affirmative action, and they wanted Pamela to help them recruit a black MBA to fill the position of financial analyst. As she stepped off the elevator and walked toward the reception desk, Pamela immediately felt the energy to be cold, antiseptic, and sterile. The receptionist was a woman of about forty with pale, flawless skin, crystal-clear blue eyes and a perfectly coifed bouffant. Pamela felt like Tom Cruise in *The Firm* when he realizes the CEO of his company isn't just any devil, it is The Devil.

As she walked through the corridors to the vice president's office, Pamela realized that each person she passed had blond hair and blue eyes. She was, in fact, the only brunette in the place, an outsider, a New York Jewish girl in the midst of a very Waspy company. Pamela felt very uncomfortable and anticipated how an African-American candidate would feel as well. Yet, on the positive side, how satisfying it would be to help facilitate one of the first non-white hires in a major organization. This would surely pave the way for other minority executives to have similar opportunities. They ultimately hired a terrific young African-American man as a financial analyst. And we'd sure love to know where he is today. And speaking of today, Andrea Jung, over forty, is currently the CEO of Avon. So truly, things have changed.

Fast-forward twenty-five years as Pamela visits the Silicon Valley office of an Internet start-up. Gingerly stepping through the trail of animal doo-doo that littered the floor (employees were encouraged to bring their menagerie of pets to work), she was instantly sorry she had worn Armani. Every employee wore shorts and sandals and worked in an extremely casual environment—one big office with no cubicles. The air was infused with a youthful feeling of anarchy, and Pamela knew instantly that it would take a certain kind of laid-back personality to work there. You would be safe in assuming that person would be nothing like Pamela.

We tell these stories to illustrate how crucial a factor corporate culture is in determining where you want to work. As we've said, the moment you step off the elevator you will feel that pulse that is a company's style. Watch how the office works. It's like observing a party. Either you feel an instant connection to the people who are there, or you feel barriers, walls put up to protect you from other employees.

Procter and Gamble, one of the most prestigious packaged-goods companies, has a reputation for being extremely conservative and bureaucratic. A close friend of Pamela's was the CEO of a company that was acquired by P&G. Pamela's friend was a dynamic woman who had helped build the company with her exceptional entrepreneurial skills, but after being acquired by P&G, she became more and more frustrated.

A burdensome bureaucracy was put in place and, during the course of three years, it became increasingly difficult for Pamela's friend to *get it done*—both in spirit and in fact. Business decisions that would normally have been rubber-stamped were caught up in a nightmarish approval process that ran right up through the corporate level. The process by which tasks were to be accomplished became cumbersome and unwieldy, with mandatory multiple approvals. Her former company's wage and salary guidelines and employment contracts were all converted to be in alignment with P&G's policies, so every time Pamela's friend wanted to promote or give a discretionary bonus to one of her staff, she needed to go through endless channels. Not only did this take away from her autonomy, but any decision took an awfully long time to process.

The merging of these two disparate cultures turned into a nightmare for Pamela's friend and she ultimately resigned. The frustration involved in trying to marry an entrepreneurial, fast-growth company with an older, established, highly structured Fortune 500 one was just too great. Of course her friends and family thought she was crazy to leave. How could she give up so much money? How could she give up the prestige? The answer was simple. She was and is an entrepreneur at heart and could not thrive in the prisonlike environment of a conservative corporate culture. She took a year off and went on a spiritual journey around the world; it was the first time she had allowed herself any time off since she had started her career. Now she is the CEO of a major company, back in a real entrepreneurial business venture.

You must determine the type of corporate culture you want. If you are an MBA looking to have a corporate experience—whether it's in finance, marketing, or operations—two to five years at a Procter and Gamble or at a company with that type of corporate culture could be just what you're looking for. A large corporation can teach you valuable business skills and methodology you would be hard-pressed to learn elsewhere. Not to mention that having a Fortune 500 company on your résumé can be a calling card for the future.

Denise Jackson is manager of human resources at the Walt Disney Company. She's the first to admit that the corporate culture at Disney can be extremely inflexible. "You must be ready to *pay homage to the mouse*," she says. "You must be willing to put your own life on the back burner, 'cause if you don't put your work first, you'll never be asked to work on the bigger and better projects. You must be ready at any minute to go home, pack your bag, and leave. I'm a corporate animal at heart. I like to know what the rules of the game are. I'm happy to learn them and happy to play them. Having come here with my eyes wide open has made the experience less painful. I'm certainly not putting in this time to carry on a resistance to corporate America. The bottom line for me is money, and I hope to cash in on this experience. I feel that every day I spend with this company is money in the bank because it translates into new opportunities in the future. There is no doubt in my mind that I will leverage this kind of corporate experience."

One of the great political lessons Meryl Holland, now president of her own company ("M" Co. & Friends) learned while in the retail business at Bloomingdale's makes for great dinner conversation. She was working in the housewares department, which, at the time, was considered the spotlight department, the area where you could platform your skills and get on the fast track. One day a man was put into her department as a second assistant, which was a surprise to her, since no one had informed her he was coming. He was a lot of fun, though, and he and Meryl got along famously. She taught him the ropes, including all the inside dish of the department: the dirt, the gossip, the bottom-feeder stuff you have to know if you want to play the game to win. Their relationship was great . . . but there was just one thing. The big boss, a great guy who happened to be gay, was in the habit of calling her second assistant every night around six o'clock. And to further her bewilderment and frustration, every Friday afternoon they would take off together to Long Island.

Finally, Meryl realized they were lovers. She reports, "I wanted to be cool, but I was completely freaked out. He was intimate with my boss, and I had shared inside information about the department that he was probably passing on to him during the weekends. In the end, he was sweet to tell me about the relationship and to make me feel comfortable about it all. My boss also confided in me. But it was a corporate culture eye-opener as to who has the inside track, so to speak."

**HOT TIP:** "Always figure out the sexual and hierarchical politics before giving away the store."—*Meryl Holland*

Jackie Young was the product of corporate America in the seventies, when a lot of the issues between men and women were beginning to surface in the workplace. As an attorney, she had status and respect in a contract law practice. But as a woman she suffered what she termed "real sexual harassment." The atmosphere was very formal and macho, and Jackie was constantly on her guard. On one occasion, a male colleague asked her to meet him for a drink at the Polo Lounge. She went, despite her trepidation, only to find that her colleague had booked a room upstairs. When she called up to tell him she felt uncomfortable, that it was inappropriate for her to meet him in a hotel room, he asked, "What do you think I'm going to do, rape you?" So, she went up, and there he was with champagne on ice, candles, the whole scenario. Jackie left the room. Two weeks later the same married executive asked her to dinner. She left the firm and its macho culture behind.

Some twenty years later Jackie was exposed to another type of *socializing off-site* when she went to work for a start-up that had a culture of studied informality. Although the business operated at a breakneck pace that was exciting, Jackie felt that the culture was more reflective of a college fraternity than a business enterprise. The dress was so casual that people came to work barefoot and in shorts, and every Friday at three-thirty there would be a beer bust that everyone was expected to attend. That's when Jackie learned the term *socializing off-site,* and her new least-favorite activity, "going to one of those places where you put on fluorescent vests and shoot each other with laser guns. I would play a virtual-reality game, my coworkers bouncing off the walls, and I would think, 'I left my office to do this?'"

You need to develop your own value system in order to match it to a corporate culture. If you are of a sober nature and don't really like to socialize with the people you work with, don't go to work at a corporation where backslapping and partying are part of the daily routine. If you are married and have children and you want balance in your life, don't commit to a workaholic environment. Don't go to work for an Internet start-up if you want flexible time at home with your kids, and don't go to a small entrepreneurial company that expects you to perform *other duties as required*. There are definite advantages to a large corporation. A large company has a lot of support systems, and your position is likely to be well defined. In a small company there will be times when you are expected to wear more than one hat and take on a variety of responsibilities in which you may—or may not—have experience. It really can be survival of the quickest and sharpest in a smaller company.

Denise Jackson ran into her biggest professional challenge when she went to work for a very small company prior to working at Walt Disney. And that's when she found her biggest reward. She went to work for a joint venture called JMA, a transportation project that pulled multiple contractors together to build specific projects. Denise's job in human resources was to form cohesive unity among a group of disparate companies, some American, some Canadian. It was a managerial nightmare—all the employees had different benefits, holidays, and schedules—but Denise had a master's degree in public administration and wanted to make use of it. That's why she originally left her digital start-up (Digital Domain) and went to work for JMA.

Denise's responsibilities may have included contact only with those people working on the public transportation system between Hollywood and Highland Avenues in Los Angeles, a relatively small distance, but her professional relationships increased by leaps and bounds. As the common link for all employees, she was in daily contact with successful professionals from all over the world. Attending to the needs of this diverse group, she found herself working with the most interesting people she had ever met: geo-techs, mathematicians, and planners. The lesson? Says Denise, "You need to be incredibly resourceful in an entrepreneurial environment, but the rewards can be great. And don't think that by going to a small company you will be deprived of mentors and seriously interesting coworkers. It can just as easily be the other way around!"

HOT TIP: Sometimes going small can increase your professional visibility.

Miramax is now a large company, but it has remained true to its humble beginnings. Although it has grown from a renegade independent film company to become a division of Disney, its culture is still quintessentially entrepreneurial. The copresidents, Bob and Harvey Weinstein, are hands-on, active workers whose corporate philosophy is based on hard work and intense focus, a mandate that guarantees the highest quality of work from employees. The Miramax-first attitude trickles down from the top. The Weinstein brothers are so completely devoted to their company and to film that they expect an extraordinarily high level of performance and dedication. To work at Miramax is to show undying loyalty to the company, put in long hours, and work extremely hard. Sign on to Miramax and you are signing on to a lifestyle where your work is your life. Most people who join are aware of this because of the Miramax reputation for quality and success. There are people who thrive in that high-pressure environment and those who cannot. Our advice is to network, get feedback from people who have worked in the company in which you are interested to determine what it is like on the inside.

HOT TIP: Culture is determined from the top down.

When Megan Barnett, formerly a vice president of Kodak, was at Universal Studios, there was a high employee turnover. Then the leaders got together and brainstormed to help make the culture more employee friendly. Explains Megan, "We just started surprising our employees and treating them. We had a surprise barbecue day. Then a surprise movie-ticket day and a surprise beach-towel day. The only people who knew the schedule were myself, the directors, and one of my employees. So people had to come to work each day to see what was coming. We did it out of fun, and that made all the difference. And because it was so much fun, we eliminated the expensive seasonal hiring cycle we'd gotten ourselves into. Employees felt more relaxed and welcomed, so they stayed."

By contrast, Megan's other employer, Kodak, was more bureaucratic and more hierarchical. "I kept asking human resources at Kodak why the boss needs to authorize a party. Kodak thinks the power is in the supervisor; Universal believes the power is with the people. Everything flows down from the leaders, as opposed to people getting together and doing it. At Kodak you don't celebrate or spend money. It's kind of 'stiff upper lip,' which is probably the Midwestern attitude. Universal was more frenetic and fun, more detail-oriented, where part of the culture is celebrating a lot."

It's worth remembering that within larger corporations, some divisions are more entrepreneurial and less rigid than others. The environment at the Internet division, for example, is more likely to be entrepreneurial than that of the other divisions. Creative divisions and on-line divisions tend to be more freewheeling than their traditional counterparts, although, interestingly enough, that, too, can be a problem.

When Denise Jackson worked at Digital Domain during its start-up phase, she likened the culture to the wild, untamed Old West. For one thing, the offices consisted of workstations in a building that was architecturally avant-garde. There were no storage or file cabinets—people would hide boxes so they could keep themselves organized—and the office was poorly lit. To this day, Denise reports, she has to wear glasses because she read so much in the dark. She describes the start-up experience as fun, though—if a little unmanageable. "It's great to put a structure in place, to brand a new entity and be part of something wildly successful. I would describe that particular corporate culture as crazy. Everything was allowed, and I mean everything: sex, drugs, and rock and roll. The company was known for its parties and proud of it. Since I was one of the eldest members of the company and in human resources, I kept myself a little distanced from other employees. There's always the old adage, 'Don't party with someone you're going to fire tomorrow.' I'm a private person, anyway; so my personality, combined with my professional boundaries, gave my colleagues, at times, the wrong idea. My behavior was sometimes misconstrued by some of the employees as cold or distant, so I would have to say my time at a start-up company was a great personal challenge."

Corporate culture is never stagnant. Even the dot-coms are changing. Fast-paced, with high turnover, Internet companies have attracted young and old alike. But the gold-rush mentality is wearing off. The emphasis now is on the bottom line, with the venture capitalists demanding a strong revenue-producing business model. Gone are the days of the dot-coms with trampolines and on-site concierges. Now Internet companies have to make money like everybody else—which is an awfully rude awakening to those who were getting used to the idea of the quick IPO and a cool ten million. It had to happen someday.

Mergers and acquisitions have put an end to long-term employment, but employees are not expendable. The job market is fantastic, and recruiters are busier than ever trying to match candidates to companies. It's a seller's market, so you have a lot of opportunity to find what you want. And that includes finding a culture that's comfortable for you. Women today are working harder, and often the workplace serves as a focus for both our personal and professional lives. Try to determine what a company's culture demands *before* you start working there. Talk to people. Find out if what they expect fits what you want to give. You must take care of yourself, and that means cultivating a degree of selfishness and self-interest that doesn't come easily to most women. Assess corporate culture with a keen eye and ask yourself *a lot* of questions. Will I get what I need from this company? Is this a culture in which I can feel comfortable long-term? If not, does it matter, if for a year or eighteen months I'll get valuable experience and contacts to use as a springboard for the next leap forward? Pay attention if the culture has recently merged or downsized. Has top management undergone change? It's not easy to maintain a cohesive culture in today's marketplace, and mergers and downsizing have a big effect on corporate culture. Self-interest has replaced company loyalty in many corporations, but pay attention if people seem overly protective of their roles or their territory. Try to assess the relationship between management and employees. If employees seem to distrust their managers, the resulting corporate culture can be hostile.

Here's a quick checklist to help you assess corporate culture:

*Environment:* Is the receptionist formally dressed and well coifed? Is she casual? Or is *she* a *he!*

*Ambience:* How does the receptionist welcome you?

*Furnishings:* Are there photographs or paintings? Is the area messy or neat? Is there music?

*Dress Code:* How are the majority of people dressed? Casually or conservatively?

*Communication:* Is there a buzz in the hallways? Are people walking around, congregating and talking? Or is there tension in the air?

*Graphics:* What is the style of the company's printed material—business cards, stationery, and so on. What is the logo trying to convey?

*Place in the Community:* Does the organization support any causes—social ones, say, or in the arts?

Some other things to consider:

- Is the company receptive to women? Are women a major element? Are women being promoted?
- Are there women in mid to upper management? If it is a publicly held company, do women serve on the board?
- Does the company support flextime should your personal life necessitate it?
- Talk with other female employees. Are they allowed to telecommute or take personal days to attend their children's school functions?
- Does the company provide for family leave and day care?
- Does the organization embrace a team approach to business? Does it foster internal competition? Is the environment overly competitive?
- Does the company have a policy of cross-training? Can you learn interdisciplinary functions that will make you more promotable?
- Does the company promote from within or hire from the outside?
- Does the corporation have entrepreneurial divisions or departments that foster independent thinking and creativity?
- What is the company's philosophy with regard to families and employees' personal lives?
- Does the company have, in some way, redeeming social value? Does it stand for something that has meaning in terms of giving back to society? What charities does it support?
- Is the organization environmentally conscientious?

- Will they pay for further education? Would they, for example, pick up your tuition so you could get an MBA?
- Do the people with whom you are interviewing have a similar sensibility and style? Is that style comfortable for you?
- What are the company's values? Do they encourage extracurricular activities? Is there a gym for the employees' use?
- What drives the company's areas of expertise? Who's at the top—and what type of background and experience got her there? It's usually a great indicator of who can climb the ladder the fastest.

Ask human resources for a copy of its company policy manual—*before* you accept a position. Never assume anything. And watch how the office works. Neil Lenarsky says that it's very important to research a company, whether you go to the web site or find an insider to tell you what really goes on. After all, you should measure the company just as the company measures you. In terms of corporate culture, the most important part of the interview occurs when you are almost through and the interviewer asks if you have any questions. Now you need to ask questions that will remove the company's mask, if you will. For example, learning what channels you go through to get something done will reveal to you their taste for structure and bureaucracy. The number of levels or steps involved reveals who's in charge and what you will need to go through to get anything done.

"Corporate structure is palpable," explains Neil. "When I walk into the MGM executive offices, I'm aware that I'm looking through bulletproof glass that separates me and the executives. I see push buttons on the doors that automatically close, which reveals that business around here goes on behind closed doors. Whereas, when I walk into Garage.com, for example, the atmosphere is very free. Everybody is walking around and talking to each other. The CEO is at the water fountain. When you walk into an office, use your intuition to tell you what the corporate culture is all about."

You must also have some understanding of who you are. When Jackie Young met Pamela ten years ago, Jackie was a candidate for a position for which Pamela was recruiting. Pamela, the wise executive-search lady, told her then that she didn't think Jackie was cut out for the corporate world, that she was too creative. Jackie was very insulted. Now, says Jackie, she's sorry she didn't ask herself what Pamela meant instead of reacting to what she heard as criticism. "It only took me a decade." Jackie laughs, but she says to Pamela, "You were absolutely right. I much more enjoy being on my own and doing jobs on a project basis, where I have maximum freedom."

Jackie moved out of a corporate job and into Electronic Arts, a company that produced CD-ROM games. She was certainly in a different culture than the one corporate America had to offer. Still, she says, it was an initiation by fire. "The culture was not diverse. It was insular. The northern Californians had a kind of snobby attitude toward the southern Californians. It was the 'Mods' against the 'Rockers,' where anyone from southern California was thought to be from Hollywood . . . that jungle of show business and puff-ball meringue.

"The irony was," according to Jackie, "as a start-up business with a young company, rich in cash and short on tradition, the culture was far more brutal than anything you could possibly find in Hollywood. That revelation was apparently lost on the young. Still, they adopted a style of management that set the standard for Silicon Valley. They took care of you. You were always being fed. There was a wonderful cafeteria, and they were always bringing in good lunches and dinners. The expense accounts allowed for great travel around the world, and the bonuses and raises were generous. Even the lawyers had stock options and were allowed flexible hours.

"In fact, the corporate culture was such that if you were in a bad mood, you were encouraged to take the day off and stay home rather than come into work and be nasty. Even though it was a macho culture, it was a liberating one. I carry some of those ideals with me today. Day care, family leave—all of those benefits were liberally awarded and thought to be the least that the company could do for their employees. They encouraged you and paid for further education, for receptionists and executives alike. They wanted you to be a part of the community, and as a result, I became very adept at public speaking, a skill I appreciate having, even now."

One of Meryl Holland's biggest lessons was learning not to feel insecure because she did not have the formal education she felt the culture required. When she worked at Bloomingdale's, she just rolled up her sleeves and worked harder than anyone else in the department and became very good at her job. From that time, she remembers a new employee, a young, very perky looking woman, holding out her hand, and saying, "Hi, I'm Kathy Winkle. I have my MBA, and I am a new assistant in cookware." She then asked Meryl to point out her new office. "You're standing in it," Meryl told her. "But this is a stockroom," Kathy replied. "Yeah, welcome to retail, honey."

At the time, Bloomingdale's was very high on recruiting graduates from business programs around the country, and Kathy fit right into that mold. "I taught her well, and when she relaxed a little, we got on fine. Reviews were coming up, and I was on the fast track to be promoted. But Kathy had her MBA. She emerged from the review, came right over to me, and said, " I knew that I made ten thousand dollars more than you a year because of my MBA, but I told them you deserved more money than me. I may have the education, but you know what you're doing."

Clearly, Meryl's educated colleague had seen how hard everyone worked and realized that her advanced degree did not necessarily translate into performance. She could talk the talk, but Meryl could walk the walk. And, Meryl adds, "It was a good lesson for me, to be rewarded by another woman's loyalty. I had mentored Kathy, and for me to understand that my experience and smarts were worth at least as much as the advanced degree gave me tremendous confidence." Kathy soon thereafter left the company; Meryl got promoted and, yes, got her raise.

• • •

Denise Jackson reports an interesting reaction to the corporate culture. She describes the culture at Disney as being very political, male-dominated, and not at all racially diverse. "Your level," she says, "determines how you're treated, what class you travel, what kind of hotel you stay in, what kind of table you get at the corporate cafeteria. As a manager, I get comfortable but not opulent travel. It's hard when you work with colleagues who are higher up on the food chain and they travel first class and stay in better hotels. How you're treated is very well defined within the culture, and you can't take it personally.

"There are less women here than in previous companies I worked for and almost zero women in higher echelons. It's a very young culture. Not many people over fifty live here. But let's face it. Disney has cachet, and it's a good thing to be able to put on your résumé.

"So, what got me here? Ego. Ego got me here. I was first romanced by the mouse six or seven years ago, but during the interview I felt no connection to the culture whatsoever, so I declined Disney's offer. The next time they came knocking, I was over forty and a little overweight. And they hotly pursued me. The thought of the number of people who would love to work here loomed, and the notion that maybe when I'm ready, the opportunity won't be here, so I'd better seize the opportunity now. . . . I don't think my being African-American had anything to do with my hiring, although I know they are very short on minorities. The fact that I had such extensive experience in the areas of entertainment, retail, and construction made me an excellent hire. The fact

163

that I was African-American may have been the chocolate sprinkles on the cake, but nothing more.

"Another change in culture. When I went to Digital, I knew they had a reputation for being high-tech entrepreneurs. Again the culture was completely free, people riding around in helicopters, using profanity. The meetings were raucous, wild parties. There were many African-Americans in high positions within the company. Ironically," Denise continues, "sometimes a start-up company has a tougher corporate culture. I remember the final straw of my days at Digital Domain, when a recently hired CFO came on board whose style didn't mesh with mine. The guy was a definite screamer, and just after he humiliated me in front of several executives, I went back to my office to lick my wounds and there was a message from someone who was offering me a job. I took it as a sign, and I grabbed the job."

Tenny Mickey, who is now the VP of Human Resources at Newscorp, worked over the years with such Fortune 500 companies as IBM, Xerox, and Bank of Boston. "As an African-American woman" she said, "I always thought I had to work three times as hard because I would think I wasn't good enough. I thought I was being seen through the eyes of corporate America—substandard education, substandard thinking, substandard processing, plus a general discomfort about having to be around an African-American woman." Her big surprise came in the form of a white male mentor who taught her to bullet-point reports and weed through data to get to the main point. "He was a very secure kind of guy," Tenny says, "preppy and very cool. He described me as a jewel in the rough and helped me enormously in my career. Had I adopted an attitude against white corporate America, I never would have been open to his mentoring me."

Tenny elaborates, "When I was at IBM, the corporate culture was stifling. There was virtually no other African-American on staff. Xerox was much more open, and they invited me across the street to come and play, so to speak. And I did. There the culture was exactly the opposite. African-Americans were thriving on staff. Other women were doing well, and they saw me as a maverick, someone they could train and bring along with the company. The management was young and diverse. Freedom of expression ruled. They did everything they could to create a warm atmosphere, and I became, under their tutelage, a very hot salesperson with lots of opportunities open to me.

"From there I went to Polaroid to work in a program in the inner city in Boston to teach working skills to the under-employed and underprivileged people. We taught skills as well as work ethics, like how to be on time. Obviously, Polaroid had a very specific value system in terms of out-reaching into the community and preparing kids, hopefully, for a career at Polaroid.

"From that kind of free environment, I retreated to the Bank of Boston, a two-hundred-year-old institution, where you would have thought the women working there should have been wearing white gloves. The rules had been on the books for two centuries, and nothing had changed. I did it for the money, the position, and the title of executive vice president. I spent three years there and used it as lever-age. What I learned was how difficult it was for me to be in a staid culture and so difficult for me to work with people who were unwilling to change. The culture housed a lot of fearful men who were pissed off and frustrated, who had no talent for courage and were always yielding to the powers that be.

"After that experience, I went on to New York and basically got my ass kicked. I was unprepared for the pushiness and the confrontations. I was lonely in the big city and went into sales, where there was no tension at all. In fact, everybody greeted each other with a big hug. It felt good and supportive and flexible in terms of my personal life."

Megan Barnett describes herself as a high achiever, very aggressive, and relentlessly competitive, and so was the culture at Pepsi, where she worked. She says Wayne Calloway, the former CEO, used to say his vision of Pepsi people was of eagles flying in formation. Well, the silent joke was that eagles don't fly in formation. They're loners, and the problem was sometimes Calloway would hire so many mavericks that they would bump into each other and it could get very competitive.

As we get older, we want the emotional energy we invest in people and companies to bring us something in return. A culture that makes you uncomfortable or doesn't allow you to do what you want can be exhausting. On the other hand, a culture that supports women and wants you to use your experience and maturity to bring in new and innovative products and services could be the corporate culture of your dreams. Check out the culture, and visit for a while. Don't hand over your passport until you're sure you want to stay.

# Chapter Six

# If You Can Talk, You Can Sell

As women we've been selling our whole lives. How else could we convince our children to eat oatmeal for breakfast, get our husbands to accompany us to black-tie events, or rally the whole family to clean up the garage on the first day of spring? Selling is convincing people they have to have something they're not sure they need . . . but will be by the time you're through with them. Think Thighmaster or microwave egg poacher.

A sales career can help you segue out of a vocational rut. Sales can be your ticket to developing a new set of skills you didn't realize you possessed and can give you an opportunity to develop a whole new career. Just think about your passions and what interests you—clothes, cars, real estate, books, jewelry, sports. Maybe even travel! There's nothing to stop you from pursuing a sales career in any of these areas. It's all about a smart approach to entry and how to take that initial step.

Terri Guitron, currently the western regional sales manager for Turner Interactive Sales, got out of her career doldrums by making the jump to sales. "I got my first job working for a very small ad agency in San Francisco as a junior advertising artist, but I got bored," she says. Terri, fortunately, was able to move internally within the agency into a media buying and planning position, where she was able to learn the new field of media buying. How did she do that? "I actually made the move through some sales reps who had been working with me to discuss media buys. And that, I think, is how a lot of people shift from the media end to the advertising-sales end. They are working as a planner or buyer and see that the people calling on them have a very good lifestyle and a lot more freedom. So they say to themselves, 'Hey, wake up and smell the coffee here.'"

Sales requires internal motivation and tenacity as well as the ability to not take rejection personally. Because selling is a relationship game, the size of your sales revenue depends on how "out there" you are. Networking is important in all businesses, but it's the lifeblood of the sales arena. You must constantly develop potential business opportunities and present a lot of new business pitches in order to close one deal. The more you network, the more people you meet, the more opportunities you'll create. In sales you never know where the next deal may come from.

One of the greatest aspects of selling is the control you have over your own income—and it's not gender biased. The harder and smarter you work, the more money you'll earn. It's really that simple. Terri says, "I don't see as much discrimination in terms of income levels for women in my field, especially on the sales end. If you're a good performer, you will be compensated in a way that far exceeds a lot of other industries."

Usually, if you are selling a product (*tangible sales*) and are employed by a major corporation, your compensation package will be structured with a base salary plus an incentive bonus based on reaching your established goal. You will also receive all the perks, such as a car allowance, entertainment expenses, cell phone expenses, and so on. Sandra Rychly, who has been in sales her entire career, says, "I think the ideal compensation is to have a base salary with commission or a bonus structure, because if you're chasing after something and you're not having revenue come in . . . well, it can be very discouraging." Sometimes it can take a year or so before you begin to realize you are building your business, so patience and persistence is key.

If you work in *intangible sales* (selling a service), your compensation package will be different. You could be on a small salary against a high commission rate without many perks. An intangible sale is more difficult because there are many factors surrounding the sale that you cannot control. Take, for example, the executive-search business, where you function as an agent—not only for the corporation looking to hire, but also for the candidate. You are dealing with peoples' careers, one of the most crucial and significant aspects of their lives. Anything can happen to prevent the match from taking place—kids, husbands, wives, relocation issues. You get the picture. The stakes are high, but the earning power is too. So if money is a strong motivating factor for you, you may want to consider intangible sales.

In the type of selling that Terri does (media time), she says, "You have to be fairly analytical. It's not extremely difficult, but it is basic math. You also have to have a flexible personality, because you're doing a lot of negotiating and getting a lot of rejection." A strong sense of self and product knowledge will get you through those tough times.

HOT TIP: When you're selling, you're trying to help somebody solve a problem.

If you really stop to analyze a typical day in your life, you would begin to see that you sell yourself in everything you do. You may be selling a project idea to your boss, pitching a new marketing plan to a client, or even convincing the dry cleaner to do a one-day special on a suit you need in a hurry. Business is about selling to clients, to peers, even to subordinates. Life is about selling too—to that dry cleaner, the mechanic, and yes, to your spouse and kids. Every interaction in which you are engaged requires you to use your persuasive and communicative skills to get what you need to get the job done. That's sales.

Consider Louise Berkman. She's our hero. Louise entered the workforce at fifty, having never worked "in business" a day in her life. Happily married and the mother of two beautiful daughters (both of whom attended Ivy League colleges), Louise was a stay-at-home mom who worked part-time as an educational consultant. With an MS in special education from Fairfield University in Connecticut, she completed postgraduate work and received a national certificate for training in creative thinking skills, problem-solving techniques, counseling, and human resources. Louise took classes over the years, but nothing ever interested her enough to pursue it as a potential career. Besides, her focus was her family and her community.

When empty-nest syndrome set in, Louise was itching to make money, meet new people, and challenge herself in the business world. She knew she couldn't compete with twenty-five-year-old MBAs, nor did she want to. She did think, though, that she should be able to transfer her academic training in creative thinking, problem solving, and human resources to the world of business. She also wanted to be compensated on merit. She believed she could produce, so she didn't want to be paid on a straight salary. Adding up all these factors, Louise recognized her career had to be in sales and marketing. She started to think about what particular industry would hold her interest, let her excel . . . and let her earn a lot of money!

Louise had some knowledge of the commercial real estate business through her husband's involvement as a real estate attorney. Her thought process went like this: *Why not start to explore an area of business in which I have some familiarity and see if I can make something happen.* And so she began her journey. She started networking within the commercial real estate business to determine what aspect of sales she'd like to work in. Would it be commercial real estate sales, working for a brokerage firm, residential sales, or working for a developer as an agent's representative? Or would it be an area called tenant representation—something that she knew nothing about. Louise says, "I had three jobs my first year. I started with a commercial broker. I was actively networking through some of my personal contacts

171

over the years, so I called a guy who was starting his own company and asked if I could meet with him. That's how I got my first job. I knew very quickly that it wasn't for me; nevertheless, I thought it would be a good idea to make an effort to meet some of the female real estate brokers in town. Through one of them I learned of this tenant rep firm. I made a cold call to the company, got myself a personal meeting, and got myself a job. I was there a short while when I realized it was still an old-boys' network and there would be no place for me to advance. Then, through a friend of mine, I found out about working for a contract furniture dealer, of which I also knew nothing. I had never even heard of the industry."

Louise learned about the furniture business through her own investigation. And again, through a cold call, she got herself hired at a furniture dealership. She could have sent a brief cover letter summarizing her educational experience and telling her potential employer how she could transfer her skills and apply them to the furniture business, and she could have followed up with a phone call to request a meeting. But Louise never bothered with a résumé. She felt it wouldn't represent what she had to offer. Cold-calling and personal networking suited her style. It got her the job, and that's what counts.

Louise joined one furniture dealership but didn't like the organization. She did, however have a good feeling about the industry. "I went to another local dealership, where I had immediate success in business development. I worked there for about a year, and then the dealership was sold. When one of the major lines, Knoll, took its business from the new company, I saw an opportunity. I contacted one of the largest

Knoll dealers in the country, and offered to represent the Knoll line in Connecticut. They jumped at the chance to expand into Fairfield/Westchester." This company knew of Louise's solid reputation and hired her to open the Connecticut office, which she actually started in the family room of her house. Within four months, however, Louise had opened an office outside of her home and had hired fifteen people. Soon she built the business into a multimillion-dollar entity.

"Through my own coming-of-age, I have the wisdom and sensibility to deal with people. I have the energy of someone in her twenties, without the burnout of all those years of work! I use my nurturing female side. I am not threatened by anyone and know that no one can hurt me. It is very empowering," explains Louise. "I see myself as a facilitator. I represent a product that people need, and I perform a service. What I give to my clients is a commitment to great service. An exciting aspect of my work is meeting great women in business. Now my biggest challenge is bringing balance back into my life, because I am giving so much to my job."

We asked Louise what type of obstacles she had to overcome as a woman embarking on a new career at her age. "You can't be afraid of rejection. Don't take it personally. People have other agendas. You need to be mindful of business politics, and sometimes you need to take a hard line and be able to confront." Confrontation doesn't come naturally to Louise, so she had to work at it. Now she finds it easier to stand her ground. "Try to be a paragraph ahead of them," she advises. "Be a good listener, and be able to communicate. Be sensitive to clients' needs. My educational background has been very helpful in this area."

Louise's journey really demonstrates how you can utilize all of your background from your personal life—your education, the people you've met through the years, your volunteer activities, and your life experiences. Some of the skills that Louise called upon to create her new career were ones she had honed just by living her life. Her ability to self-start, for example. From her teaching and educational-consulting background, she had outstanding verbal and communication skills. She had the distinct ability to listen to her clients because she had been a mother (who listens more than a mother?) and had taught children over the years. She had the ability to negotiate, developed from years of running a household. And because of her desire to succeed, she was extraordinarily persuasive, tenacious, and patient. She knew not to take rejection in business on a personal level. Louise is a living case study of how you can successfully launch yourself on a different and exciting path.

HOT TIP: You are selling *yourself* first and foremost.

If you apply for a sales position and possess any of these traits, there is a strong likelihood that you will be hired without having had the "required" experience. But you have to be convincing. You have to demonstrate that you have what it takes, so that your future employer will go outside the proverbial box. Refer to your past work record and your extracurricular activities. Wow them!

"When I was working in San Francisco," Terri Guitron says, "I had a woman friend who was a schoolteacher. She had no sales experience, and yet she became one of the highest-selling salespeople in the San Francisco marketplace. The company I worked for hired her because she had tenacity and really good verbal and written skills. I would definitely hire someone from a different field, although she would likely have to start off in a more junior position. If she didn't have traditional advertising experience, but perhaps had a sales background with a good track record and demonstrated communications skills, I might put her in a sales-planner position to get her to really understand the business."

And suppose you are an accountant who is tired of running numbers and sitting alone in the back room not talking to anyone all day? Could you segue into sales? Absolutely. First, you could try your current company by networking with some of the salespeople and developing key relationships. If you recall, Lynda Lytle did just that at Xerox. Ask if you could tag along on a sales call or attend a new business presentation. You'll be surprised at how receptive they will be to this type of interest. If you are unable to get transferred into the sales division, then start to look on the outside into a nontechnical industry like publishing (selling advertising space for magazines, newspapers, or an Internet company) or real estate. You won't have any technical knowledge to learn, so it will be easier to enter the playing field. Having accounting skills will give you a leg up in negotiating and putting deals together because you understand how the numbers work. You can read a balance sheet and profit-and-loss statement. You'll also have a lot of other pertinent information in your bag of tricks. No one can pull the wool over your eyes in a negotiation! So you could use that as leverage when presenting yourself to the decision makers. Deal making and negotiating skills are integral to closing a sale. You want to emphasize how significant your financial background is coupled with your people skills. This double whammy makes you a great package that would enhance a sales department.

Don't forget to make use of all the intangible assets of being female. As Terri says, "I think what we bring to the table is our listening, intuitive, and analytical skills. Unless you are going after a highly technical product line, you are unlikely to need training. A woman with a business background, self-confidence, and a keen awareness of people, not to mention some intuitive negotiating skills, can definitely learn to sell."

Local radio sales is also a great place for women with no sales experience. It's an industry that is personality driven, so if you have good presentation skills and an outgoing demeanor, you are eminently hirable. Selling advertising time to local companies to advertise on local radio stations gets you some good sales experience under your belt and a transferable skill to parlay into the next job for more money and a more senior position.

The hottest place to be today is, of course, the Internet. Selling banner advertising for an Internet company or for the web sites of cable or network properties is an in-demand job. The industry is still relatively new and in its pioneering stages, so getting in the door is less difficult than in more established industries. The Internet is today what the cable industry was twenty years ago, so if you've got people skills, can think strategically, present yourself professionally, and are filled with enthusiasm and energy (remember how important attitude is), go for it!

The on-line industry needs your experience because so many of the founders of Internet companies are young, with little or no corporate background. Again, age is in our favor. One media company we spoke to said that their intention is to hire more seasoned people who can develop strategic partnerships with major corporations in the so called "old economy," where the executives are older and more experienced.

So continue to utilize your female advantage and your age. Promote the skill sets that make you a valuable human resource. Hear what the other person is trying to say, because when you're selling, you're trying to make your product solve somebody's problem. That's why you're there.

# The Internet

If we asked you to give us a composite description of a successful Internet entrepreneur, you'd probably give us a profile of some hacker with pizza boxes piled up outside the door of the garage that houses his start-up business, someone who years ago would have been on the FBI's Most Wanted List and is now on the cover of *People* magazine as this country's Most Eligible Bachelor. But there's another type of Internet success story, and it's not about a guy at all. It's about a woman who's seen forty, a woman who grew up in a nonelectronic world pounding typewriter keys and swearing every time the carbon paper stained her hands. She didn't buy a computer until she bought one for her teenager. And she didn't use one until her husband left his unfinished solitaire game up on the screen and she placed the last ace. Savvy and practical, this woman knew there must be more on the Internet than card games and quickly proceeded to on-line shopping and services to make life easier. Back then, she hadn't thought of applying her professional skills to an on-line position—yet now that's just what she's doing.

From Silicon Valley on the West Coast, to Silicon Alley in the East, women are running full companies from a home or car that has been newly equipped with a cell phone, fax, and pager. They beep and hum as they walk down the street, appearing to talk to themselves as they close some megawatt deal. And they will tell you that since technology unwittingly tore down the corporate ladder, the Internet is the first level playing field the girls have shared with the guys.

The stock market may consider the Internet to be the most volatile thing since the crash of 1929, but it's not going away. Great news for us, because the new frontier is in desperate need of women. Men may be more interested in the details of the technology, but it's the women who are concerned with putting the technology to use. The potential link between the computer screen and philanthropy and community activism is perfect for women interested in social change. It's also great if you want to make a buck. (Not to mention that it's probably less demanding and more supportive than the man you married—and will never hand you an unmatched sock and ask if you know where the other one is.)

The Internet is a great frontier for rebels. Managers of Internet companies are looking for people who have experience going up against the system, who can handle chaos, take risks, and operate in a no-structure zone. Who better than the Woodstock generation to leverage their peace-marching skills, roll up their tie-dyed sleeves, and march into Silicon Valley, older but wiser warriors. And we have plenty of female representatives.

Nancy Saslow and Carolyn Carmines are the founders and co-CEOs of PushyBroad (standing for *pushed and broadband* content) a television, interactive television, and broadband studio (broadband is high-speed Internet access via cable, telephone, or satellite). Nancy and Carolyn provide one-stop shopping for content and design across all media, creating original material for television, interactive/enhanced TV, broadband, and narrowband (narrowband is content delivery at a slower speed). They also package content for clients across every platform. Coming from traditional backgrounds in broadcasting, Nancy and Carolyn were, in their own words, "gripped with fear" when they jumped off the secure gravy train of company benefits into the Wild, Wild West of the new technology. They chose the name PushyBroad (a fabulous marketing tool, if you ask us) to send a message to the community at large that not only did they intend to have fun, but they were here to stay, thank you very much. "We wanted to hearken back to the time of Katharine Hepburn, Lauren Bacall, and Rosalind Russell, when being called a 'pushy broad' was a compliment," says Carolyn. "Men love to kid us about our name, and PushyBroad is a brand they have no trouble remembering." It's also subliminally seductive. Says Nancy, "I mean the rules have become such that no one is quite sure what it's okay to laugh at, so we're kind of a breath of fresh air. We laugh at ourselves first, and we find that many of the men who deal with us are not as guarded or as threatened." Nancy adds that "humor doesn't diminish credibility—it underscores security and confidence. The name doesn't diminish the quality of our work or the seriousness with which we carry it out. People embrace the name Pushy-Broad. Both men and women love it. Once you hear the name PushyBroad, it's hard not to laugh, and it allows people to lighten up. At one conference, Gerry Laybourne, CEO of Oxygen, was so impressed by the branding she put a Pushy-Broad sticker on her lapel. She got it!"

We asked our trailblazers if it was easier for them to take this leap of faith into a new career in their forties? "Absolutely," says Nancy. "We never would have done this in our twenties. We would have been way freaked out." Carolyn adds, "As women, we don't have a lot of venture capital behind us, so we have to have trust in ourselves. That's easier when you're older."

The best part of the new frontier for women thirty-five-plus is that Internet start-ups don't necessarily require large amounts of up-front cash. In the case of PushyBroad, Nancy and Carolyn set a specific time line and budget for themselves, since neither of them was interested in starving to death. They both understood that women tend to deny themselves to make a business work, so even though they agreed to put some of their personal needs on hold while they devoted themselves to making their business financially profitable, they agreed from the outset to set a time frame. That helped to take some of the pressure off. PushyBroad measured its success by the way it took care of its staff and vendors, and by the way they were able to pay themselves. Taking care of their people was key.

Each of them invested in the business, since there was no angel money or outside investors. Nancy had run her own independent film, TV, and video-production company prior to partnering with Carolyn, so during the initial start-up phase, PushyBroad worked out of her small office. Nancy and Carolyn realized that they didn't have to become IPO millionaires in the first three years, nevertheless they were definitely motivated by profits. And while money was tight, they enjoyed creating their own corporate culture. Carolyn says, "We both dressed to go to the office, but we had a choice. If we were seeing clients, we would dress differently than if we were just working at the office all day. I am the Ann Taylor type, and Nancy's more Eddie Bauer. She loves to wear her sweats." Or as Nancy's mother used to say to her daughter, "A little lipstick wouldn't hurt."

HOT TIP: If you are an account rep who wants to break free of daily visits to your clients, the Internet may be for you.

If you're a woman with no time for a personal life, you can't beat the lifestyle. We all get to a point where working in physical solitude is preferable to dressing up and commuting downtown. And there is plenty of opportunity for Internet employment, both by leveraging skills and by learning new ones. Think about leveraging your skills by finding a hot growth industry. See what job listings are posted on the web—start with Monster.com, jobs.com, HotJobs.com, Career.com, Headhunter.net, and Futurestep.com. For example, research what the company offers in the way of e-commerce, dovetail your contacts and experience with that specific e-commerce opportunity, and parlay what you do now into an Internet job. If, let's say, you want to work on the administration and office management side of an Internet company, research the companies that are the Internet equivalent of your brick-and-mortar background. And don't forget: Consider only those companies that are philosophically aligned with what you want to do and who you are. This approach works for operations, distribution, finance, and marketing too. Take your old economy experience, find the Internet equivalent, and follow your Career-Emergency Marketing Plan to a new position.

That's what Jamie Fragen did. Now the e-commerce Manager at Expedia, a division of Microsoft, she had longed for the challenge of a new career in the new technology, as well as more time to raise her young son. A former nine-to-fiver who went panning for gold, she made out like a bandit! Several years ago Jamie had the foresight to take her marketing and advertising skills to Microsoft, initially developing marketing and sales opportunities for clients in the e-commerce business. In a very short time, she was promoted to developing West Coast business for Expedia, a primary travel portal on the Internet. She spends her day surfing the Internet, analyzing revenue opportunities within the hotel, rental car, and airline category. And now she leaves the office around five to go home and have dinner with her family, because after she tucks in her son, she can work from her laptop if she needs to.

In terms of starting over, Jamie agrees with the founders of PushyBroad that the entire Internet business world needs and wants women in their prime. Says Jamie, "The best thing about women in the Internet is that there really is no good-old-boy's network yet. In fact, the old-girl's network has the edge because we're so good at networking. The more we know each other, and the more aggressive we become about it, the more capable we become of helping each other. I have found that women in the Internet business are very inclined to work with each other and network more strongly than women in other industries."

And what about the "voodoo" of the new world? Jamie continues, "Confidence is much more important than technical knowledge. I believed in my ability to deliver. I wanted to change careers and knew I had to convince whoever was hiring that I could do it. Believing you can do it shows strength and willpower. If you believe you can do it, the employer will believe you too."

Tina Sharkey knows that the Internet is all about timing. She has been in the right place at the right time . . . several times. Tina was fortunate to have a mother who was both her role model and her mentor. When Tina was in high school, her mother, president of Perry Ellis America, was in a position to encourage her daughter to come to her office and sit in on meetings. One of the people she "luckily" met at her mother's office was Tomio Taki, chairman of Takihyo, the company that owns Anne Klein and Donna Karan. At that time, Tina was working at her first job in sales in the garment industry. She had asked her mother what the fastest track was to become a CEO. Her mother had told her that sales was one of them. Tina says, "There I was in the office of this shogun-like man, and I was just fresh out of college in this *schmate* job totally thinking, 'What did I need an Ivy League education for to do garment sales?' And there on his desk, like an omen, was a picture of a video vending machine. As it turns out, when I attended the University of Pennsylvania, I wrote a business plan in cooperation with local vendors for this exact video-tape vending machine." Was Tina in the right place or what?

In the middle of all this excitement, in rushed Donna Karan, the Queen of Fashion, swathed in four cashmere blankets. It was the middle of summer, and Tina thought she was in the middle of a movie set when the chairman asked her a million questions about the video product. Tina began outlining the strategic advantages and disadvantages of the business. Says Tina, "In ten minutes I found I was more stimulated than I had ever been in selling any spring line. And the next morning they hired me, even though I talked them out of the very investment for which I had written a business plan. Instead, they had me look at a little business which interested them called 'high-definition television.'" Tina was hired as the vice president for marketing and business development for Rebo High Definition Studios, a pioneer company in HDTV.

"For five years I launched new products and got involved with the film industry—all as a result of a little picture on someone's desk. And that's the message. Don't be shy. I could have seen that picture and not said anything. God knows I was intimidated when Donna Karan flew into the room. But I decided to speak up, and it lead to a new career.

**HOT TIP:** There's no track for success in the Internet business. You make your own!

On the subject of the Internet, Tina says, "Women's opportunity on-line is enormous right now. First of all, in cyberspace everyone is an underdog, so it doesn't matter who you are. It's really about how you apply yourself to the medium. The Internet is all about confidence and being a curious, independent thinker. I don't like to play by anyone else's rules. I don't even read the rules. I don't read manuals. I just plug in and start pushing buttons, and if that works, then great. That's how I feel about life as well. There is no manual. There is no track. And if there is, I don't want to be on it. I don't like being measured by other people's standards."

You'd think the Donna Karan, picture-on-the-desk-story would be the ultimate coincidence, but it's not. Tina elaborates, "I was living in an apartment building where Children's Television Workshop was also housed. One day there was a fire, and I ran out of the building. It was a freezing day in February, and I went into a coffee shop to wait until I could go back." Tina continues, "I ran into a woman who was also waiting, and it turned out she was a professional friend and the chief financial officer at CTW. We had formerly worked together at Q2 [a lifestyle shopping channel]. After talking a bit, she asked me what I thought should be their Internet strategy. And in short, she introduced me to the CEO of CTW and they hired me. I was the president of on-line services at CTW [Children's Television Workshop], which meant I oversaw all of our Internet strategy—our multiple web sites and all of our distribution deals along with America Online and Excite and Web Crawler. I was also involved with experiments we're doing with WebTV and a whole host of partners."

Tina was one of the pioneers of the Internet. Early in her career she worked for one of the leading strategic communications agencies, Frankfurt Balkind, as senior director of client services, concentrating on strategic planning, corporate identity, and communications services to entertainment industry clients. It was there that she met Barry Diller, who was her client and had recently created the renowned electronic retailer, QVC. Barry Diller had recruited a woman named Candice Carpenter to run the company. He introduced Tina to Candice, and Tina became the first person hired at Q2, their lifestyle shopping channel. Tina spent two years there, first as their vice president of marketing and ultimately as their vice president of programming. Candace left Q2 before Tina and subsequently asked Tina to join her to start iVillage. Tina became the senior vice president of programming and chief architect at iVillage, where she was an original founder of what is now a household Internet brand. Tina oversaw the development of the company's media properties—across all distribution platforms. She also led the company's business and creative development efforts in extending its brands to other media, including books, syndicated newspaper columns, games, and television. Tina also developed the ChatVillage Network, the Internet's first personalized community network with member-generated content at its core. Currently Tina is the founder and CEO of SocialMedia, an Internet advisory group.

Tina says, "My advice to break into the Internet boom is this: In order to have a position on the web, you have to use the web. You cannot show up at a job interview for an Internet position without an e-mail address and some surfing time under your belt. It's stupid. Period. It kills me when people come in on their high horses because they feel that they're so accomplished, and yet they've never even used a search engine. You have to think of the Internet as a level playing field: a whole new thing. Once you start, you can start laying over skills. But you have to start."

The key positions in an Internet company are COO (chief operating officer), CTO (chief technical officer), CMO (chief marketing officer), CFO (chief financial officer), senior vice president of business development, and senior vice president of advertising sales. If the company has an e-commerce component, then they would need to include a senior merchant or merchandising manager. If it is a content-driven web site, then they would need to hire an editorial director. In terms of skill sets, it helps to have a direct-marketing background. Direct marketing in the off-line world is the process of identifying certain groups of people in terms of psychographics and demographics in order to contact them directly with a marketing message. Some of the tactics of direct marketing begin with accumulating or purchasing lists of names, addresses, and phone numbers. These lists may be of magazine subscribers or credit-card users, which are then matched up to the consumer. Direct-marketing methods include direct mail, telemarketing, direct marketing with direct-mail promotions, invitations to events, or a sample product.

The Internet is the purest direct-marketing medium ever invented, since it allows you to directly aggregate people with similar interests. Companies now have access to information based on on-line surveys, purchasing habits, and registration data that indicate individual needs and interests. Extremely valuable. The technology provides data mining services research that can then be utilized to directly market to the consumer. Look at Amazon.com. It's a great example of how the Internet can be used to reach the consumer directly. Say you've ordered a beauty book from Amazon. You are now recognized as a beauty-book reader. Because you are registered on the site, Amazon has information about you, including your e-mail address. They can e-mail you book suggestions and tempt you to purchase more books. When you click onto Amazon.com now, the site will be personalized for you, complete with product recommendations. This is quintessential one-to-one marketing. As Internet executive Robert Hollander says, "One-to-one marketing is the Holy Grail of e-commerce."

**HOT TIP:** You can leverage any skill you have and apply it on-line.

Women with editorial backgrounds can reinvent themselves on-line, but first they need to learn how to apply their skills in a different way. The Internet requires good communication skills, but if you have come from a magazine or book publisher, you'll need to reinterpret those skills because the platform is not the same. Yes, the Internet requires good writing, but it's a different kind of writing. It's all about sound bites. It's all about immediacy. Content-driven web sites like iVillage.com, WebMD.com, Garden.com, and all of the news and sports sites need people with editorial backgrounds to select from the massive amounts of information available. Why not you?

We know we've told you this, but we want to emphasize the point. If you're thinking about entering this business as a second career, don't be intimidated by the computer itself. No matter how far we women have come, we're still programmed to think that all that hardware stuff is for the guys. Almost every woman we spoke to in this business admitted that though she initially felt threatened, she eventually asked enough questions and read enough books to realize that the new technology is in fact very much like the Wizard of Oz. Once you get behind the curtain, you see that it's a lot of smoke and mirrors. The new frontier requires a set of skills you can learn like anything else.

One woman we spoke to with a key job in this technology told us she had been scared to death of the technical mumbo jumbo when she started. But every day she taught herself something new. And every day she asked questions of her colleagues, who helped her through the fear of learning a new language. One day, she realized she had actually gotten a reputation in the company for being the computer nerd-genius. Seated on an airplane beside a techno-frustrated male colleague, she was asked by him for her help in fixing his computer. Secretly delighted with herself and without missing a beat, she smiled, took his computer, and in a matter of minutes fixed the problem. And never once mentioned that she worked in sales, not technology. So, ladies, no more complaining about the flashing 12:00 on your VCR!

## It's All About Passion

The biggest piece of advice we have for you, should you want a new career on the Internet, is love the Internet. Surf the day away and really develop passion and energy for this magnificent technology. If you're not in awe of what the Internet can accomplish, then you're probably better off using the e-commerce sites to buy a bathing suit at three in the morning.

## RESEARCH THE NEW TECHNOLOGY

Have some understanding of the landscape and the competition out there in cyberspace. Use e-mail every day. Investigate the search engines and web sites. Pick up some trade publications and a copy of *Wired*. Start experimenting with different sites, and don't go back to all the familiar ones. The Internet is like a Chinese menu. Try something new, besides the vegetable fried rice.

One woman who hires for the Internet said that she wouldn't even consider hiring someone who didn't have her own web page. It's not that complicated to design, and if you want to switch gears into the new technology, that may be a realistic and demonstrative goal.

## BE WHO YOU ARE

The technology may be new, but a lot of the old rules still apply. You still have to be plugged into a network of your peers, you still have to have a solid and honest reputation, and you still have to work hard for your clients. If you have been a COO of a consumer-products corporation and want to try your hand at an Internet start-up, you will still be hired for your industry knowledge and managerial skills, not to mention your expertise in running a company. Carole Ference is a successful woman who has spent her career as a publisher of major magazines—*House Beautiful, Town & Country,* and, most recently, *Live! Magazine.* She is currently a partner in an on-line start-up company, utilizing her publishing background in an Internet space. Instead of attracting readers, she goes after the eyeballs. And just as before, she builds strategic alliances with major corporate advertisers and taps into her managerial experience to help her younger staff. If you are a vice president of marketing in a major retailer and move on, you take your marketing skills with you. These skills transfer from a brick-and-mortar company to the Internet. There is no magic here. It's still the same old world where you have to look both ways before you cross the street and where you have to ask your kids three times to clear the table. Even though it seems as if everything is in flux, it isn't. It just feels that way. The new technology needs people with flexibility and adaptability. Because you have to constantly think on your feet and be ready for the next new BIG idea, the new frontier is looking for renegades with an adventurous spirit who can take their personal and professional past right into the new millennium.

HOT TIP: Be confident. The industry is in its infancy. No one is looking for someone with ten years of Internet experience.

Think of your past jobs and careers as the raw material for a gigantic collage. If you've spent some time in advertising, sales, publishing, or even journalism . . . now's the time to mix it up and put it on your server. That's the beauty of the Internet. You can finally take all the pieces of your skills and experiences and combine them into a creative whole. As Jamie Fragen reminds us, " I find that women thirty-five-plus want to marry their passion with their purpose in life and really combine both things. I personally have learned through default, through trial and error, that I like to sell. I like to deal with clients. I like to be strategic and creative. I took those interests and skills into the Internet travel business, and in a couple of years I may want to do something that allows me more flexibility."

The Internet abounds with opportunities to be creative in relationships and in deal making. The barriers are down. People who were previously not connected are now finding themselves in board rooms and garages shaking hands and making deals. Suddenly the hybrid of entertainment and new technology is a whole new business unto itself. Working in this technology is a little like fixing up your old college roommate with your newly divorced neighbor. You're trying to make a match, a marriage, as it were. And it's all so new. The businesses that are suddenly merging have to write their own vows.

## Weigh the Personal Advantages

We bet no one asked you about the quality of your life when you first started in the workforce. Well, now it's a deal breaker. For Jamie it's crucial. "I have a five-year-old and often leave the office at five o'clock, go home, and have dinner with her. After I put her to bed, I get on e-mail and work again until ten o'clock. And it works for me to be home on certain days if I have to. The good thing I've found about sales and the Internet is that management is less inclined to pin you down to a location as long as you're making your numbers. If you prove you can work and make your revenue, you can obtain a certain level of independence and autonomy. It's you and the client, as opposed to you and the team."

## IF YOU CAN SELL, YOU'RE HIRED

One of the biggest needs for an Internet company right now is sales, and frankly, if you've had any work experience at all, we're betting you can sell. Everyone doing business on the Internet is looking for people to sell advertising. Sales is something you can learn, as long as you are personable and have a lot of energy. If you can think on your feet and you like to talk, all the better. We don't know one girl between us who doesn't like to do both—at the same time.

And again, as we keep telling you, it's an advantage to be a woman. As women, we're earning more than ever before, and retail companies are desperate to get us in the door or on the site. According to Jupiter Research, women over forty have the highest income, but less time to do anything, than any other demographic on-line. We are the peanut butter of the sandwich generation, the group that's pulled between the needs of our children and parents, always looking for a simpler, more efficient way to cross off items on our extensive to-do lists. The point being, it takes one to know one. You know what women need because you are one, and you know how to sell to women because you know what works. As of the year 2000, fifty-one percent of all Internet users were women, so believe us when we tell you that companies need you. All those years of asking: What do women want? And men are still clueless. That's why one man's apathy is another woman's paycheck—in every retail arena. Traditionally, cosmetics companies and clothing outlets have always come after us. But now, automakers, insurance companies, and financial services are addressing us as valued customers, thank you very much. Even sports equipment manufacturers and toolmakers want us.

Internet companies are so desirous of staff that they'll help you meet your professional goals. The good thing about a company like Microsoft, for example, is that it provides a lot of training, which you can support by going to the library or logging on to Amazon.com or Barnes & Noble.com and finding some really good sales-training books. It's a brand-new world.

## DON'T BE SCARED BY SOMETHING NEW

It's good to know "just enough" to be dangerous. One of the things you need to learn is how to put together resources and find people who are skilled in the areas in which you are deficient. And hook up with others. That's what a good manager and a savvy woman does well.

## NETWORKING: AGAIN

Sick of this piece of advice yet? Networking is mentioned in every chapter of this book because the opportunities created by networking are endless. Jamie Fragen is in a technology group called WINT (Women in New Tech), which has offshoots such as YINT (Yenta in New Tech), AINT (Asians in New Tech). "I can pick up the phone and call any of these women . . . ask them anything," explains Jamie. "I can be as naive or as bold as I want to be with my friends, and that's really special. We all help each other and refer business to each other."

• • •

If you're thinking that you're too old for such a new and young technology, you're flat-out wrong. Even though the culture is new and innovative, the road to success is generally accomplished in the old-fashioned way—lots of networking, marketing, lunching. Nothing earth shattering. Several years ago, managers at Internet companies thought they didn't want baby boomers holding them up with silly questions about PalmPilots and downloading. But in fact, Internet companies are finding they need veteran managers who did it the old-fashioned way and actually know how to build a corporate infrastructure. Baby-boomer women have survived some of the most turbulent times of this modern, downsized, merged, and acquired American workplace. Start-up companies need smarts and flexibility. After the glass ceiling and equal pay for work of equal value, start-ups are a piece of cake.

Says Lisa Crane, former president of Soundbreak.com and the former vice president and general manager of NBC.com, "The Internet is always evolving. Females are used to adapting quickly to change. When you're dealing with a system that's constantly in flux, you can't afford to have male cockiness around. Women over forty are more interested in ongoing learning for learning's sake . . . that's the Internet." Lisa continues, "What I love about the Internet business is that it's surf and turf, a real combination of arts and business. Family and freedom were big issues to me and I wanted both. I also wanted the freedom to participate in some charitable work. And I wanted my company's blessing."

Pamela and Nadine had to ask the founders of PushyBroad (you didn't forget the name, did you?) if there's a spiritual component involved in quitting cushy jobs for the huge adventure of a start-up company? "Sure," they say, smiling. "We pray all the time for new business, and from all faiths. Whatever will bring in more business, that's the god we pray to."

What's the bottom line? If you have marketing experience, the Internet is a natural second career for you. Your skills will transfer right to the on-line business because you're selling right to your old friend, the consumer. If you are an account executive at an advertising agency, your skill set of managing corporate clients and dealing with the various departments within the agency lends itself to the areas that would be involved in the marketing of an on-line company. If you are a brand manager in a Fortune 500 company and are responsible for strategic marketing and brand building for a consumer-goods company you can transfer those marketing skills to an Internet company. The same principle applies to the planning and buying of media. As well as the jobs of creative director and copywriter, especially if they are in the broadcast industry.

The important thing to remember is that women who understand the consumer and who know the demographic of the end user can transfer any skill to the Internet. For example, someone who is in the magazine business knows consumer marketing. They understand who is doing the buying. Similarly an editing or publishing background is very transferable to the content-development areas of the Net.

There is a tremendous need for ad sales people. Any sales background can transfer over. If you can talk with confidence and product knowledge, you can sell. You need to know how to cultivate relationships, negotiate deals, and close them. But you can come from a field totally unrelated and transfer the people and negotiating skills to a new industry.

Although the World Wide Web (the commercial face of the Internet) is only a decade old, there are still some companies looking for second-generation on-line experience. Don't let this deter you. We believe that if you have the industry knowledge you can still take the leap over to the Internet side of your industry. With the right relationships and off-line experience you can make the move to the Internet—provided you combine persistence with some time surfing and talking to friends who are already working for Internet companies. The Internet is like any other business, especially now after everyone's realized that you don't have a license to make money just because you're a dot-com. Keep that in mind. Just be ready to pull apart your skills so they are separate and functionally recognizable. Research the targeted company. Then apply your skill sets to whatever business model you're going after and specifically to the needs of the company or the organization you'd like to work with.

Meg Whitman, who is the CEO of eBay (where we spend way too much time collecting white pottery), had no Internet background. But the venture capitalists hired her because she was an expert marketer. Having come from a background not only with Disney, but with packaged-goods companies as well, they needed her to brand the eBay name so that it would be recognizable to the consumer. In this case, she surrounded herself with executives with technical and Internet expertise, and has had great success.

You can transfer almost anything you do to the new technology. But first you have to buy a computer and use it! Now available in many pretty colors . . .

# Chapter Eight

# Mind Your Own Business

There are now over eight million women-owned businesses in this country. A little bruised from hitting the glass ceiling and weary of inflexible hours and making money for someone else, these eight million women have struck out on their own. They're running family firms, moving into nontraditional fields such as automotive design and road construction, and increasing their presence in traditional lines such as catering, day care, and media. And they're employing one out of four workers in the process.

More businesses are targeting their services to women, and more women are enjoying the thrill of economic power. What better way to create that power and to act out your control-freak impulses than to start your own business? And what better way to enjoy it? The thought of starting your own business is romantic. We all want to be the boss, the one to lead the team and come up with the great idea. And we all want to be on the receiving end of the profits. But it's risky not to have that regular paycheck, to do without the support staff and the expense account. And whom do you call when the computer crashes? You do know you have to have a great idea for your product or service. And you also know that you have to have a first-class business plan. But have you given any thought to what else you need to consider before you stop punching the clock? There are some things you should keep in mind.

If you're a risk taker and think you can paddle your way through the ebb and flow of your own business, fine. But if you're the kind of person who lies awake at night worrying about your outstanding Visa balance, taking this plunge may not be for you. Establishing your own business is like a roller-coaster ride. Be prepared for a feeling of exhilaration, followed by a panic attack when a voice (yours) screams, "What was I thinking?" Most of the women we spoke to say that it takes about eighteen months to balance the manic highs of newfound freedom with the depressive lows of isolation and loneliness. Ride this out and you'll be on your way to becoming a true entrepreneur.

For Karen Juarez Boyd, starting her own business meant she could free up more time for satisfying her soul as a community volunteer and, hopefully, recover from a severe case of corporate burnout. Explains Karen, "I was really tired. I kept thinking, *Where should I be? How am I tracking?* I thought I was where I wanted to be, but I wasn't loving it. I was not the person I wanted to be.

"What did make me happy was volunteering for the blind, which I had done three years ago but stopped when my job became too demanding. It was frustrating. I had always felt that once I reached a certain level of success, I could pursue the things that made me happy. But I was still under the gun. One day it dawned on me . . . *all I do is work. If I dropped dead today, what have I done? What have I contributed?*

"So I got off the treadmill and used my experience to go off on my own as a start-up business consultant. After I established myself, I followed up with my game plan to do community work. My clients include corporations from industries like cosmetics, pharmaceuticals, biomedical instrumentation, opthalmic devices, and banking.

"I became a volunteer, teaching interview and business skills at an organization downtown. Many of the people I taught were former prison convicts who were unemployed due to drug problems. My goal was to teach them skills and to help them get their self-esteem up to the point where they could lead some kind of a normal life. Now I'm in a mentoring program for girls in protective custody who, for whatever reason, can't be in foster homes right now. I tutor a little girl every Wednesday night, and I've become her best buddy. So once a month we do an off-site visit. I take her places. It's fun and I love it.

"The truth is that in the corporate world no one was supportive of me being out in the community or putting my time into boards. Establishing my own business was, for me, a way of regulating my work life. Now that I'm in charge of my own business, I'm also in charge of my personal life. It's wonderful. My biggest piece of advice for women who want to transition into their own business or to work at home is to establish professional *and* personal goals. A younger woman at my office once confided in me she wanted to have children, but was afraid that if she did, it would throw her off her professional track. I told her that I was successful, that I had graduated from Yale. I had stayed on my professional track, but didn't have children. I advised her to think hard about what she wanted—professionally and personally—and to try to establish balance. If you're smart and you work hard, your career will be there. Other opportunities may not."

## Do What You Know

Think about taking skills that you already have and profiting from them at home. Sheree Mitchell, from Columbus, Georgia, had been a registered nurse for eleven years and knew from being a single parent how difficult it was to find quality day care. Using her reputation in the community as a healthcare worker and her considerable experience with children, she dived off the deep end, took out a loan for $1.2 million, and built her first child development center, Growing Room, Inc., in 1989. She began with 250 children and today has 750 children enrolled in that day-care center and two others she has since built. Say's Sheree, "When you start your own business, the demands are high, but once you make it, it's a joy. I like watching my employees grow, and I love that I'm doing good things for children. Businesswise, once you're successful the first time around, it's easier to get money from the bank. When I went to build my third center, it took me ten working days to get a loan of over a million dollars. A track record."

Linda Livingston was a teacher with two children who got tired of going on family vacations and dealing with messy suitcases and kids who had no idea where they'd packed their stuff. Weary of being the designated the "lost and found," she developed her own line of compartmentalized gear bags with labels so everyone would know where to find their belongings.

Linda couldn't even draw when she began her endeavor. She had to use an instruction book so that the drawings she sent to the manufacturer weren't too stick-figurish. She explains, "I hired a sewer and a pattern maker. I didn't even know I needed a pattern maker. Then I hired a publicist, and then another mom knew someone who did marketing in New York. All of a sudden, through my network of soccer moms, I was on QVC. Now, I'm my own shipper, secretary, and writer.

"In terms of capital I was pretty nervous. I had no financial backing. We took out a second mortgage on our home to do our first production. We're not wealthy people, but when we went eighty thousand dollars into debt, my husband was really, really supportive. And luckily, within six months I was able to turn a profit. The advice I would give to any woman looking to start her own business is that, believe it or not, there are things out there that we have not thought of to make the world a perfect place. So if you hit upon an idea that no one else has thought about, go for it."

## Design a Business Plan

It's vital to have a strong business plan. Describe your proposed business in detail, emphasizing the importance and uniqueness of the product you are selling or the service you are providing. Use real numbers to prove why your business should succeed. Be realistic or even conservative when it comes to numbers, but don't be shy when it comes to recounting your experience. Make sure your potential backers know what you bring to the table.

Here are some things to consider when drafting your plan:

- Who is your customer?
- Who or what is your competition?
- What will your start-up costs be? Don't forget permits and licenses, phone lines, and all relevant equipment.
- What are your operating costs? Overhead? Utilities? Stationery? Detail even the smallest expenses.
- Think about your cash flow requirements.
- If you are dealing with a product, what is your distribution plan?
- Think about your marketing angle. Can you market from home?
- Can you live without drawing a salary for a year?

Freaked out? You may want to enter your new business part-time or moonlight with the security blanket of a regular paycheck and health benefits while you're trying to establish your new endeavor.

## Capital

The good news is that more banks are lending money to women who want to start their own businesses. Over forty-six percent of women-owned businesses were able to get institutional or bank financing during 1998 and 2000. If you're thinking big, see if you can find a financial partner or investor. You can start with friends and family, but bear in mind that borrowing from people you know can be tricky. An invitation to dinner from an investor who is also a friend may feel more like a past-due notice than an offer to share a meal and a bottle of wine. Make sure to document your agreement in writing. And be realistic with your repayment schedule. Your income stream depends on many things, not the least of which is how fast your customers or clients pay. In figuring out your needs, know that the biggest downside to starting a small business is the difficulty of collecting money for services rendered or products sold. Larger companies often don't pay on time. This is the biggest complaint of independent contractors—male and female. Keep it in mind.

## Market Yourself

You are now the CEO of your own company, free to put your feet up on the desk. So let people know. Posters, flyers, and business cards will help you brand and advertise. Then network, network, network. Find other companies that complement your own for possible strategic alliances, and make yourself known to them. When Pamela first began recruiting in the entertainment field, she "gave away" one candidate without charge so that her client would understand the value of her service. Now that's marketing!

# SETTING UP A HOME-BASED BUSINESS

## Space

As Virginia Woolf wisely advised, every woman needs a room of her own. You need a separate work area for your home office. Clean out the garage or the spare room that you've avoided cleaning, and treat yourself to a new desk. You absolutely need to get your own work phone line with an answering machine attached. Having your two-year-old or your mother answer your work line seems a tad unprofessional. And you need child care. It's impossible to work from home and actively look after your children. The idea that you can is a mommy-track myth conceived and perpetuated by someone who's never been around children. Don't be in denial. If you're going to work out of the house, you can't also be cutting up little pieces of apple and performing magic tricks. No one will take you seriously.

**HOT TIP:** Don't set up shop in a corner of your kitchen, otherwise last night's lasagna will settle into your keyboard and file folders.

## Off Limits

Make sure your friends and family know when you're working at home and when they're allowed to disturb you. Everyone in your life has to be clear about your office hours. Just because you're home doesn't mean you are fair game for social contact or chores. People have an uncanny way of thinking that if you're home, you're available to pick up the cleaning and takeout Chinese food. Speaking of which, you may want to lock your refrigerator door during the day. Several women who work at home told us they gained five to ten pounds from the nervous munchies—which could be enough to send you back to your boss begging forgiveness and a sugarless environment.

## PJ Alert

Clearly if you have clients visiting your "office," you will want to look as professional as possible. Even if no one will see you, it's best to forgo the pj's. So get dressed. We know the heavenly fantasy about staying in your jammies and not washing your hair, but there's something about that level of casualness that can get depressing without your even being aware of it. When you look in the mirror and think that a *schlump* alien has taken over your body, you know it's time to take a shower and face the world, fully clothed.

## Contact

Make sure you keep up with your colleagues and continue to attend seminars and lectures in your field. Otherwise you can get isolated and people will forget you're out there. And don't forget the printed business cards, letterhead, and brochures. Remind people you are still on the planet.

## Technology

We can't stress enough that you need to get wired. Completely. And say good-bye to dull grays and beiges. Indulge yourself with a computer in one of the many luscious color choices.

## Relax

Women report that when they first start working out of the home, they work harder than when they were in the office. You are allowed to get up and take a break, a walk, eat lunch. It's okay. If someone calls, well, that's what the answering machine is for.

Judy Barker, who has a background in finance (she actually ran Unocal's philanthropy area for a while), was looking to have more fun. So Judy, a good cook, concocted a formula for essential body oils. She realized that a lot of people get those little bottles for gifts and don't know what to do with them, so they just sit on the shelf. She thought that putting aromatherapy in a body oil lotion would be an effective way of getting those essential oils into your life on a daily basis. A woman could apply them right after her shower and fill the whole bathroom with a lovely aroma in the process. A nice way to start the day, if you ask us.

Thanks to the woman who runs the lab where the products are now made, Judy was able to launch her line. "She has a scalable facility," explains Judy, "so that as I grow, she can grow with me. That's really our first sell, because no one wants to work with the little people. There's not much money to be made until you grow and are ordering larger volumes. My angel investor believed in the concept and the product, so she's been very collaborative through the development phase. She also threw in her graphic designer, who charges by the hour, to work with me on packaging, so it's been a wonderful relationship.

"I've suffered a lot of fears. I think there's a lot at stake in terms of my ego. But I've set a time frame—six months—for it to be a go. I'm in production right now, and then it's going to be guerilla marketing. Either the consumer will fall in love with my product or she won't. So the fear is financial. Even so, it's less about the money than it is about pouring my heart and soul into a venture that I really love and believe in. Unfortunately, I can't really talk about my product because it's too touchy-feely. No one in the finance-and-investment world is going to take me seriously if I go into a lot of detail about my aromatherapy business.

"This is the first thing I've done where, if it really takes off, it's for life. As long as this product sells on the shelves, I'm here. This is nothing like a corporate job. You may get a regular paycheck at a corporation, and you're marketable elsewhere, but the day you walk out the door, that's the end. I believe in myself. I can sell. I can work with manufacturers. I can create a product that's beautiful, one that I think people will want to buy. So why not me?

"I set up shop in my study with a phone and fax. I'm out at meetings a lot and at the lab, so I'm not in my office all the time. I love the flexibility. I don't mind talking calls even when I'm in the shower. In my whole corporate life I wouldn't have dreamed of taking a call unless I was sitting at my desk with my pen and paper to take notes. It's psychologically very refreshing for me.

"My advice to women who want to start a new business? It takes courage, but there's an incredible amount of support out there. There are a lot of small companies who want you to succeed, who were where I am now five years ago. Everyone wants to walk into a department store and see your product on the shelf and say that they were involved with the creation of that product."

HOT TIP: "Anyone looking at starting her own business should have an eye toward the growth potential. Don't necessarily stay with what's comfortable. Make sure you start something that can grow with you into the future."—*Judy Barker*

Kathy Unger spent years as a political consultant working for Congressman Mel Levine of California and then at her own company, where she played with the big boys and girls. She had a partner, major clients, and a big staff—but was tired of all the fund-raising. So she gave up most of her clients and moved her office into her home. Now she works with major corporations trying to enhance their image in the community. She works with billionaire Paul Allen's company and with the Annenberg School for Communication.

"I'm not so emotionally involved," Kathy explains. "It's not like ruining the environment or anything. It's not a social issue I feel strongly about. I'm not working with, let's say, Philip Morris. No one's killing anyone, so I don't have to have a point of view."

She has a little wing off her house with a little bathroom next to it that happens to be the powder room. She can close the door and be away from the rest of the house. She has a separate office line and admits that "even when I'm walking through the house and the home phone rings, I do not pick it up. I consider myself to be at the office. Period. The biggest disadvantage of a home office? Meetings. I don't feel comfortable saying to a client, 'Come over to my house.' To me that's unprofessional. So I go to the client, or we meet in a restaurant.

"The other thing I don't like is doing my own filing, but it's not like I really need support staff. I can do a contract. I do my own research. I don't do that much paperwork. And with e-mail, I don't have to use messengers or FedEx. Years ago I felt that there was a stigma attached to working out of the home. Now I don't feel that way. A lot of people choose to work out of their homes, and I don't think that brands you as a dilettante. But it used to be that you weren't taking life seriously, that you weren't a professional person if you were working at home. So I would say, have the courage to try. Many small businesses don't need much capital to start. Try to start your venture with your own money, or finance it yourself. Then you don't have to answer to anybody. That, and make sure you have your very own computer. Don't allow your office computer to be the family computer."

Jackie Young could have made a six-figure salary in a fancy law firm, but chose to work out of her home instead. The reason? She likes to work in cycles—say, between 6 AM and 2 PM—then shut off her computer and go to a midday movie. After that she often comes home and works until midnight. The home office situation suits her independent nature entirely. The only drawback, she claims, is getting up early to deal with the East Coast. "I can get a bit fuzzy," she admits.

When Meryl Holland left the corporate world to run her home office, she was newly married with a baby. "I always knew I wanted to be out on my own," she says, "and I was used to working for start-up companies, so why not my own?" To make the transition easier, Meryl brought her long-time executive secretary with her, so that she could focus solely on her clients. "If you can finance your assistant, do so. Since you're not in an outside office, you're not as plugged in as you once were, so you're not getting the information you used to. A good assistant can schmooze for you, as well as deal with the beginning rush of business and administrative details. That frees you up to deliver to the client."

Since Meryl has a great work ethic—very disciplined, very focused—she found the hours agreeable. In fact she often works at night after her child is asleep. "Between nine to eleven PM is my best time." She works out of a redone garage, a comfy space that's separate from the house. The nanny and even my husband know not to come in when the door's closed. Leaving the corporate world has given me much more time with my child. In fact, every minute I don't have to spend commuting is an extra minute I get to spend with my child.

"I've also found that since I'm working out of the home, I try to find clients who don't need a lot of structuring and nurturing. I'm best," Meryl admits, "with a client who's looking for a business partner, someone with whom I can round out what they can't bring to the table. It's less hand-holding when I can contribute as an equal."

Overall, if you're fed up to the teeth with bad bosses and feeling trapped by a nine-to-five prison schedule, then starting your own business may be for you. But don't forget that being on your own can increase your anxiety level, and you may end up working more hours—but in a much more comfortable setting. After all, there's no place like home—even if it's your office too.

## WORKING FROM HOME

We're called telecommuters, virtual staffers, even moonlighters. What we have in common is a telephone, a fax, an improvised filing system, and the family pet. Not to mention a life.

We're women who have moved our work into our homes because we were tired of sitting on busy freeways commuting to an office. We're women who want more control of our lives and our schedules. And with big corporate layoffs and a big boost in technology, we've figured out how to work and be home for the repairman, the cable guy, and sneak in a little *Oprah Winfrey* on the side.

Few of us have an interest in pledging our heart and soul to the competitive world of corporate America. We're more concerned with balanced lives than balance sheets. Now, as mistresses of our own domain, we can have satisfying work, right alongside flexible work hours, creative child care, and an occasional all-girl's lunch. No wonder home business has become big business.

According to the U. S. Department of Labor, women with children under the age of two comprise the fastest growing sector in the labor force today. So, clearly, unless you work for a company with a family-friendly policy, flextime, and/or day care, the only solution to the problem of working full time and raising children is to work from home. Some forecasters believe that thirty to forty percent of workers will soon be operating full- or part-time from a home-based office. Having been treated so badly—discriminated against, underpaid, and toyed with by the watercooler—for so long, we've evolved. We've learned how to be tough and independent. Survival of the fittest, baby. And as for all those guys who gave us a hard time for having children . . . well, they unknowingly created a new breed of shark—the woman who works out of her home.

For many companies, having telecommuting employees is more economical than maintaining a fully staffed office on the premises. Since there are no distractions or office politics, the worker can get more done. You can work when you're the most productive and make up time instead of being stuck in the car for an endless commute. It's a myth that if you work from home, you can be on-line while helping your toddler build a Lego rocketship or have a neighbor drop by for coffee-klatch gossip. You must be very disciplined and set up and maintain clear boundaries: your children must be in school or day care, your friends must know not to call about sales at Neiman's, and if people ring your doorbell soliciting money for some cause—just know they're part of the reason there's a five-day waiting period for the sale of handguns.

If you want to work from home and stay with your present company, you're going to have to convince someone in charge that not only will this increase your productivity, it will save the company money. Know going in that living and working in the same space has its own set of challenges. But it's the new millennium and the day of the virtual office is just beginning to take hold. Over the next decade, as the working world adjusts to new technology, corporations will develop a new attitude toward their workers. Managers will become less hands-on and more facilitative and supportive of their enterprising entrepreneurial workers in the field. Hard to believe, but there will be a manual for working at home available in every human resources department. Not possible you say? Then who could have imagined computers, flexible hours, and casual-wear Friday in the days of the button-down shirt and the two-martini lunch?

## The How-to on Working From Home

Submit a proposal detailing specifically what you're going to accomplish from home and how you're going to do it. You need secure data transmission from home to the main office. Address the issue of interruptions, explaining that interruptions at the office will not be replaced by distractions at home. Find a "rabbi"—someone high up in the company who's supportive of employees working out of the home. Designate a young up-and-comer (preferably someone you mentored and with whom you've established a relationship of mutual respect) to be your eyes and ears, to keep you aware of anything you need to know and any last-minute meetings that you need to attend—either in person or by conference call.

Your manager or boss will have to trust that you're loyal and dedicated. This is something you'll continually have to demonstrate. Plan to come into the office at least one day a week so you can check in. Keep in touch with everyone at the office by e-mailing your schedule and keeping colleagues up to date with your projects. Save e-mails for an electronic paper trail. Schedule regular appointments with your boss and your team to keep up with the job, and reassess your arrangement on a regular basis. Is it working out? Be aware of attitude shifts. Do people treat you the same as they did before you worked from home? Listen to what your "eyes and ears" person has to say. Then take her to a great lunch, and make sure you bring along a gift. You're not above groveling.

The person that does best working out of the home is self-motivated and cooperative, a real team player—someone who knows how the organization works, so they always know whom to go to or call on. Otherwise you will get the reputation of office princess—someone who needs pampering and special attention. Don't isolate yourself in your castle.

Donna Richmond has been working out of her office for TNT Media for ten years. She buys program time on television from her home in Las Cruces, New Mexico, while hooked up to her company in Los Angeles via modem. "It began," she says, "as an experiment. Once I proved I was disciplined enough to do the work [they can tell by the dollar-amount billed], it was acceptable.

"I pretty much sit down at the computer by eight or eight-thirty AM and work until about eleven-thirty AM. I walk to the kitchen for lunch, and then go back to work. When my children were young, I sent them to day care even though I was technically 'home.' It's too hard to work when you have a toddler running around. You can't give them the attention they need and deserve.

"I like working at home because I hate the commute and I'm distracted at the office. When you work at home, you don't have all of the socializing, people walking up to your desk and observing you do something. I don't like office politics, and I don't like personality conflicts. I don't like that people complain that someone didn't say good morning or that the guys made the coffee too dark. There are office politics no matter where you work, and that drives me crazy. At home, I don't hear about it. People will leave the company and I don't even know."

Still, working out of the house isn't for everyone, as Colleen Griffin will attest. "When I first tried working from home, my office was still in the house and the boundaries would get crossed. One thing that drove me crazy were the neighborhood gardeners. Everyone on the block had their gardening done one day a week. I'd be on the phone and I'd hear this guy with a blower going, and I just couldn't shut it out. I never adjusted to working from home. I remember on the first day of my job that I got up, put on my makeup, and did my hair. Then I realized I didn't have an office to go to, so I got into my shorts. Going to an office makes me feel that I'm actually in business."

Alice Yardum-Hunter is an immigration attorney who works primarily out of her home. "My home office began out of crisis," she says. "I had been working with a very famous immigration attorney when suddenly, everything in my life was in turmoil. My relationship ended. My daughter started a new school. My aunt died. My au pair wrecked my car. It was a horrible time, and my employer wanted more out of me than I was willing to give. She wanted me to be 'her savior.' That's a direct quote. I just couldn't do it. I was a single mother with a house in Tarzana and a kid in private school, and I was not seeing my child because I was working so hard. I had tremendous expenses, and felt I was between a rock and a hard place. I was forty-two years old. So there I was having a mid-life crisis and I severed my partner relationship. I thought I wanted to go into another field, but then I realized I loved immigration law. I had just never given it everything I had. So I went out on my own.

"It's been interesting. I miss the interaction. I have colleagues I can call whenever I need to, but I miss the daily thing of walking down the hall and speaking to another attorney in the office. So I make sure I keep up my networking. It's very important to have a network of people in my profession, people who I can call to bounce around ideas. Otherwise, I'd become too insular.

"It's important to make your home a well-organized, aesthetically pleasing environment, so that it motivates you. I have my computer set up in the corner of a room that has two windows that join one another, so I'm looking outside all day. I also love having the dog around. I think that's been very helpful. I am self-motivated and self-disciplined. I begin my day with a morning walk. Then I shower and start working.

"The essential part of a home office is having the confidence in yourself to know that you have what it takes to do the job. If you don't have that kind of confidence, you probably should not be working for yourself. You've got to know your stuff. You've got to make sure you keep getting educated. And then, let go of the little things that don't always work out." Life's a lot like that.

# Chapter Nine

# Dream Jobs

It all makes sense. Now that women are pursuing second or third or even fourth careers, we finally want to do something we've always dreamed of. For so many years we did what we were told or what was expected of us. We may have supported a family, chosen a career right out of college, or perhaps we just settled for corporate security and benefits until we were afraid to leave. But in the end we did leave.

We talked to some women over thirty-five who made the big leap to make their professional dreams come true. Interestingly enough, none of these women were concerned with the almighty dollar. They followed their hearts and their passion to do something with their professional lives that ultimately affected others, pursuing a career in which they could jump out of bed in the morning, look in the mirror, and say to themselves, "I am making a difference," or, "I am finally doing what I always wanted to do, and my own life is pleasurable."

If you find yourself depressed and reaching for the chocolate, if getting out of bed to go to work is getting harder and harder, then you must begin thinking about how to end that destructive cycle. Start now. Ask yourself, "If I could do anything in my life, what would it be? When I was a child, what did I dream about? What is it that I could be doing part time right now that would give me insight into how to make my dream come true? Could I attend lectures or perhaps join charity organizations that would put me in touch with likeminded people who could help me pursue my dream?" And finally, "Where did my dream get derailed? What do I need to help buy back my soul?"

Here are a few inspirational stories to help you find your way.

## FROM PRODUCT MANAGER TO FILM BUFF

Pat Zdunowski was a product manager at the Chase Manhattan Bank for over twenty years. On the surface, it was a dream job—good pay, international travel, exciting projects. Often she was in some foreign and exotic land working on what she once would have thought were satisfying pursuits. Pat had what the rest of the world regarded as a fabulous job. And yet, with all of the excitement and all the perks, she wasn't happy.

Like a fish with a bicycle, Pat felt her natural place was not in the world of business. From the time she was in college, she had a passion for the arts. Even with her intense work schedule she had countless theater subscriptions. Often she would attend three movies in a single weekend, frequent museum exhibits, and while away her leisure hours in book-stores reading about her first love—film.

Calling home one day, Pat discovered that an old friend from school had died at age forty, leaving behind two small children. All she could think of was how she hoped that her friend had done the things that she had wanted to do, that she had not put any dream on hold. Pat says, "I just started thinking how short life really is."

Aware of her passion and the ticking clock, Pat began noticing little things at the office she hadn't noticed before. She became aware that her interests hardly meshed with those of her colleagues. On the wall near her desk, for exam-ple, Pat had hung a bulletin board filled with posters of Ian McKellen from *Richard III* and postcards from her exotic travels. Not one person ever commented on that bulletin board. Pat found that odd. The culture was restrictive. Every-body talked numbers, not books or theater. People moved through the halls like automatons motivated by the bottom line. Not one person seemed to be interested in the uplifting beauty of a watercolor or sculpture. The watercooler conver-sation was always about Wall Street tycoons, never cutting-edge filmmakers. Pat realized she no longer valued what her colleagues valued. Her professional walls were crumbling. Pat needed another plan.

Pat had to be honest with herself. She wasn't climbing the ladder at the rate she should have been. She was smart and a hard worker, but since there was no joy in Mudville or, in this case, Wall Street, she knew she could never achieve greatness until she went where her heart belonged. Pat was passionate about the film world, but there was still the practical issue of getting a job in the narrow field of entertainment. The Hollywood D-Girls are very young women, usually fresh out of film school, who get paid slave wages for the privilege of developing material for top producers. But Pat had never wanted to act or to direct.

**HOT TIP:** "Anyone can do a yeoman's job, but to be really successful and to make it happen, you have to think about work all the time. Let it occupy you constantly."—*Pat Zdunowski*

The lightbulb finally went off in 1991 after Pat went overseas on a project. When she returned to the office after several weeks away, Pat had to wait until her boss handed her another assignment. This was the first time this had ever happened; usually her projects were assigned back-to-back. Now with some time on her hands, she began moonlighting. She began her part-time exploration of the film world and thought it would be wonderful to see independent films with other people who loved movies, who could later discuss the films in a roundtable format.

Pat began to research film-buff groups, but before long she was handed another project and was back in the grind at work. Her hours were long, the recovery time hard. She couldn't bear the ethical conflict and pressure that went with looking for a new career on the bank's time, so instead she would retreat with her Chinese takeout and watch television, just to unwind. Pat's anxiety and depression grew, and before long she became a poster child for the stressed-out, middle management banker whose soul has been denied for too long.

One day, sitting in a Johannesburg hotel room, Pat's New York manager called to discuss an inconsequential situation. Gently asked about some kind of deadline, Pat hung up abruptly in a snit, overreacting to a "nothing" request. At that moment, it became clear to her that she could no longer be a banker. She could not live without professional gratification anymore.

Pat flew back to New York and gave two weeks notice. Immediately she was consumed by a kind of fear she had never known before. She had always lived in a world of benefits and a steady paycheck, and for the first time she was out in the cold, on her own, surviving by her own wits. Pat suffered an almost phobic physical reaction, developing a constant shakiness and a feeling that her whole body was encased in plastic wrap.

The ritual of leaving her professional security blanket almost made her faint. At her exit interview, the bank unceremoniously cut Pat's ID card in half. After signing the papers and giving back her office passes, Pat walked back out on the street with a dull ringing in her ears, her heart pounding in her chest. She was almost paralyzed with fear. She could hardly leave the house. Her friends worried about her. But after weeks of hibernation and emotional paralysis Pat decided that if she didn't give her dream a try, all this anxiety would really add up to nothing. So she came out of it with a vengeance, throwing herself into her new venture. She networked like crazy, calling everyone she knew and asking them to put her in touch with anyone they knew in the film business. She went to the library and researched film groups around town and figured out there was nothing like what she wanted to do, in terms of an independent film forum.

She called her business the New York Film Buffs, and for the first season she sent out flyers advertising the five or six films she would present and then discuss. At first, none of the producers she approached would give her any films to show. It was April. Her forum was scheduled for January, and she had not one film in hand. Pat had hit her first brick wall. She begged. She hounded anyone with connections to filmmakers, even becoming friends with a producer's mother to acquire an independent film. Desperate and up against the deadline for the deposit she had already made on a screening room, she called the Sundance Institute, which profiles independent films, and schmoozed some nice young kid over the phone. She sweet-talked him into faxing her a catalog and, faster than you can say "Mrs. Robinson," proceeded to book as many films as she could from their roster.

The angst of starting a business was overwhelming, and often Pat found herself wishing that her childhood dream had been to become a nurse instead of an artist. Still, she feels it was worth it to throw herself out there and finally experience the freedom that her soul so badly needed. Pat's new business was about more than film. It was about making her lifelong dream come true.

Unfortunately, Pat had to close up shop on her film business. She was having fun, but not turning a profit. She's now working at an Internet start-up company doing product placement and very happy to be conducting business in a corporate counterculture. When asked why a bunch of twenty-year-olds hired a woman in her forties, Pat explained, "They liked that I had banking experience. But more than that they liked that I had taken a risk in the independent film world. It didn't matter to them that I hadn't succeeded. It only mattered that I had put myself out there and tried." A good lesson for all of us.

## FROM FLIGHT ATTENDANT TO BED AND BREAKFAST PROPRIETOR

Doris was a flight attendant with United Airlines for twenty-six years. She loved her work—serving passengers, making them comfortable, anticipating their needs—but she also knew that the time would come when she would feel too old in a young person's business. Being on your feet all day drains your energy. And all that traveling dries out your skin. We won't mention the airplane food.

But Doris wasn't ready to retire. She loved working and wanted to find another professional outlet, another way to enjoy her affinity for the "people business." She gave the matter some thought (a lot of thought, actually), and decided that her talent for making people comfortable and safe could just as easily be employed on the ground as in the air. And that's how Doris came to establish a bed and breakfast in Martha's Vineyard, where her family has lived since the 1800s. Now four years after her retirement from United, Doris runs Twin Oaks, a five-room, Dutch colonial bed and breakfast that is filled to capacity. Last year she billed $100,000 worth of business from a house that pays her mortgage and her bills with enough profit for a good income. The great bonus is that she created an apartment at Twin Oaks for herself, which greatly reduces her living expenses. Seems the talent that once took Doris around the world has now brought her home.

Doris worked on buying the property and setting up her license three years before she stopped flying. The overlap was a blessing. As she made her applications to the zoning office, she was sued by a white neighbor who did not want Doris to open up a black-owned business next door. Open about her racial attitude, she wrote Doris a letter suggesting she establish her business in Oak Bluffs, a primarily African-American community on the island. After an exhausting and ugly three-year fight, Doris won. But had she not started preparing for her second career three years before her retirement, that battle could have cost Doris her dream. Of course, being of a certain age, Doris had the skills and confidence to fight the good fight with support from her neighborhood. But she endured a vicious personal attack, and during the court proceedings she couldn't sleep or eat. Ironically, however, Doris developed great inner resources. Even though the lawsuit cost her thousands of dollars, she persevered and became a much stronger person, as well as a community leader.

Doris loves being in charge and having total control over her own business. Proud that her guests enjoy a happy and comfortable stay, she derives great satisfaction from knowing that she is in charge of their journey, from beginning to end. But there's more. When she started her second career as an innkeeper, Doris had never been married. She had always told her mother that she was too busy, that if some man was going to marry her, he'd have to show up on her front porch. Guess what happened? Five years ago, a friend of one of her guests visited Twin Oaks, and he and Doris fell in love. At age forty-eight she did indeed marry a man who showed up on her front porch.

Doris advises women who want to make a career switch to do something they know, or have a flair for. It's her belief that going back to school and being trained to do something completely different is not a great idea because it cuts into the time you'll have left to do something else. She also thinks you should be transitioning into your new career at least three years before you leave your old one. Whether it's by volunteering or getting your financial life in order, slowly begin the move. Don't stop everything to make an about-face. Take time to prepare.

Doris also suggests that your second or third career be something in which there's no room for ageism. Had she kept flying, even though she was good at it and it paid well, Doris felt that the stereotypical image of the flight attendant who is twenty years old, with blonde hair and blue eyes would not have meshed with who she was, a late-forties African-American woman. "At a certain point in life," says Doris, "some things are not worth fighting."

Should you have a dream of opening up your own bed and breakfast, remember this: Running an inn is a twenty-four-hour-a-day job, and you're it. The plumber. The decorator. The cook and complaint department. Everything. But, Doris says, "You get great personal returns. I am currently the president and one of the founding members of the African-American Association of Innkeepers International. I love encouraging more African-Americans to go into the innkeeping business; it's immensely rewarding." After so many years of traveling, Doris's wanderlust was more than satisfied. Now her longest journey is from the attic to the first floor. A trip she makes a hundred times a day with great pride and satisfaction.

## From Broadway to Bali

Sheryl Sciro was a Broadway actress—a little bit of television, a little bit of a musical gypsy—when she won a scholarship with Stella Adler and a place in the original production of Tommy Tune's *Stepping Out*. Unfortunately, the production closed after three months, and she was out of a job. Sheryl had no experience with anything else. All she had was a desire to perform, wanderlust, and a great voice.

Around this time, a friend was starting a spa referral service and looking for actors who were articulate and sympathetic—able to speak well, able to sell services over the phone. The job paid eight dollars an hour, and Sheryl could go to an audition any time she wanted. It was ideal. Many of the people calling the service were dealing with difficult personal issues—obesity, divorce, some kind of professional or familial loss—so the company required people who were skilled communicators, people who could be articulate about what the spa could offer. Sheryl was perfect. She enjoyed the work and soon became so proficient that her salary was raised to ten dollars an hour. A fortune when you're a starving actress. And then one day she came into work and discovered that the owner of the spa had died, leaving Sheryl unemployed and a business very much in debt. "It was one of those crossroads" she said, "where you think, *This has nothing to do with me. I'll just go on and be a gypsy.*"

But, instead, Sheryl decided to jump feet-first into the spa business and see if she could swim. She even brought in her young soap-opera husband and several of her actor friends to work with her. A good actress, Sheryl believed that if her band of gypsies could take over the business, they could also play the part of being good at an entrepreneurial venture. It turned out to be an Academy Award performance. Using a little skill and a lot of bluff, by the end of their first year they paid off a $35,000 debt that the owner had accrued. Sheryl's boss had been very wealthy, and he had approached problems by throwing money at them. The starving actors' brigade was different. They redid the business using as little money as possible, but focusing on a high-quality spa experience for each customer, which resulted in people coming back a second and third time, and spreading the good word to future clients. Soon their customers were relying on them to send them to the best spas all over the world. Today, Sheryl has a multimillion dollar business with employees who travel internationally in search of the perfect spa, not to mention a television show called *Spa Finder* for Fox's Health Lifestyles. And everywhere she goes, she is given the royal treatment: the best massages, the best facials. Her new office even looks like a spa. And now that she represents over two hundred spas worldwide, her company has become the largest wholesaler to travel agents.

Sheryl jokes that her current lifestyle is about as far away as you can get from the Bohemian life she used to live, where owning a VCR was considered a capitalist offense. But she enjoys her great success and takes pleasure in supporting other women, often hiring women over forty because she believes that having a mature attitude and an experienced personality really helps boost sales. In fact, she tells a tale of hiring a woman over forty who had never worked outside her home a day in her life, but had spent some twenty years taking care of her parents. Sheryl realized that this woman knew the stresses and details of everyday life, and that her experience as a caregiver meant that she had empathy in abundance. She gave her a chance. Now this woman travels all over the world with a job that gives her full benefits. And, because Sheryl has invested so heavily in her—her new-employee training program is extensive—she knows she'll get a good return. "Because of my own background as an actress," Sheryl says, "I recognize that the people who can do this job come from diverse backgrounds, generally in theater or travel. Age is on your side in this business because we're all part priest, part mommy. You have to be able to open people up and have the experience to be there for them when they do."

**HOT TIP:** "Never settle. Ever."—*Sheryl Sciro*

Sheryl's advice to women who want to change careers is, "Think about how you want to make a living. The more enthusiastic and passionate you are, the better you will be at it, regardless of your age. Life is not a dress rehearsal. You may be too old to sing like Pavarotti, but nothing is sexier than doing what you love to do and having grandchildren at the same time."

# FROM PLAYER TO PERFORMER

Pam Sherman was a high-powered lawyer in Washington, DC, an up-and-coming litigator on the fast track of a very powerful Washington "insiders'" firm. But Pam knew there was more to life than practicing law, so as a way of satisfying her long-burning desire to become an actress, she began performing on the side, just as she had done in college with a double major of international relations and theater.

Although she was remarkably successful as a lawyer, Pam had always thought of her practice as a way of making a living—a tad better than waiting tables like other starving actresses. Pam was very industrious in her off-hours. She did late-night theater so it wouldn't conflict with her time at the office, and she did some commercials on the weekend too. "My partners were always stopping me in the hall and asking me if they had seen me in the Marie Calendar cookies commercial. I enjoyed that."

One day, out of the blue, her law firm dissolved. Suddenly, Pam was without commitment. And a job. She received three solid offers from prestigious legal firms, but emotionally, Pam was just coming to terms with the fact that she hated practicing law. So she kept some long-term clients and decided if she didn't go out there to discover if all the world really is a stage, she would regret it forever.

By her own admission, Pam didn't exactly become Meryl Streep. She began her career with voice-overs and appearances in industrial training films. She did anything that came along, including some very bad theater. But, she says, she was so starved to work at her chosen profession that even performing bad theater felt great. After a stint at the World Bank translating in order to make ends meet, Pam finally received her Equity card. Her dream come true. And when she was hired for a show called *Shear Madness* at the Kennedy Center, her mother could finally say, "See that girl up there on stage? She used to be a lawyer."

Performing eight times a week was a fantasy realized for Pam. Her advice to the endless number of women who have always imagined being asked to prepare for their close-up? "At a certain point, if you're receiving any kind of a paycheck in acting, then you have to be willing to leap off the bridge." When she was doing voice-over work, for example, Pam would say to herself, "Well, I'm not a star. I'm not in New York or Los Angeles. But I work regularly. I attend acting class. I do some pretty good theater work, including women's theater, and as it turns out, now I'm applying my lawyer skills to my acting career." As an actress, Pam is not dependent on an agent or a manager to make her deals. She writes her own contracts, negotiates her own pay, and sends notes out on any impending contract. "Once," she recalls, "I had signed on for a job in Las Vegas and they had promised to pay for my airfare from New York. When I actually received the employment letter, they had somehow forgotten to include my perk for free travel in my contract. So, I fired them off a legal letter, only too glad to remind them of their legal obligations."

Pam has tremendous respect for her peers. They show up on time, they know their lines, and they hit their marks . . . every night. On her side Pam's chutzpah factor coupled with her legal background has helped her in her new career.

Recently, she received a fifty-page script on Monday, memorized the entire document, and was on camera with it by Wednesday. Pamela laughs and says, "It's why I work all the time. I remembered all those torts and precedent cases from law school days. Now I remember lines, and the producers and directors know I can do it." Any surprises? "The thing that really surprised me was that at a certain point, my dream job became a job. You just can't walk around in a fog, and say, 'Oh, I've got my dream job.' Every dream job has tedious aspects and everyday details to attend to that make the dream part very much a reality. What is still so dreamlike is the passion and excitement and energy I have for the work."

Maybe Pam will never accept an Oscar, but there was one moment when she knew she had made it. She looked out in the audience and saw her former law partner sitting there wearing a navy blue suit with a tie. And there she was, up on stage, having herself a ball, doing improv and living it up. Even though she wasn't making as much money as her former colleague nor had his financial security, she was having a blast. She was having far more fun than he could ever dream was possible.

## FROM HAIR CARE TO HORTICULTURE

Even Cheryl's first job had to do with making the ordinary beautiful. She began as a cosmetologist, but was forced to quit after three years to look after a terminally ill in-law. When that responsibility ended, just before her thirtieth birthday,

Cheryl knew in her heart she could not go back to her old profession.

Through an employment agency, Cheryl got a temporary position at Redmond Hair Products. She loved the company, especially the way the employees were treated by their boss, Tom Redmond. "Everyone received excellent benefits" she says, "and often Tom would shut the whole company down for what he called a cellulite break: a recreational period with rolls, coffee, and free microwave popcorn." Redmond would also conduct boat days when he took his entire staff out on a lake for a leisurely day off. His company was filled with little perks and courtesies, to the extent that each employee would receive an additional one-hundred-dollar bill when Redmond had a particularly good month.

Not only did this company encourage Cheryl's career path, but Tom Redmond became a permanent role model. The fire was lit under her right then and there, and she resolved that someday she, too, would own a company and treat her employees the way Tom Redmond had treated her. Cheryl says, "The employees were so loyal that even when they bought supplies to make and test the various hair formulations, it was as if they were spending their own money. The employees really cared about the products they were using and that, in the end, the Redmond name would be on that bottle."

Cheryl started at Redmond in production, packaging shampoo in boxes. Even though she wasn't challenged, she knew immediately that she loved this corporate culture and wanted to stay. She also knew she wanted to move to another position. Cheryl took a look around, which she was encouraged to do, and decided that she would like to formulate new products in the laboratory. And in the way of a true family-friendly company, Redmond sent her back to school as part of its employee-incentive program. Redmond's policy was to cultivate loyalty by retraining its employees and paying for them to further their interest and involvement within the company.

The family-type atmosphere at Redmond was wonderful. Everyone knew everyone else's husband and kids; they even saw Cheryl through a painful divorce and, eventually, a happy second marriage. Her supervisor's philosophy was to put family first, to take some time to think about what you really want, and, above all, make yourself happy—a lesson she was about to put to use yet again.

While working at Redmond, Cheryl used to jump out of bed and sing show tunes in the shower. Unfortunately, her husband was dragging himself to a job he didn't like. Cheryl was committed to making this new marriage work, so after much discussion and mutual soul-searching, they agreed to explore their shared passion for landscaping by buying an existing landscaping business. Her husband would run the business, and Cheryl would contribute her efforts part-time.

Cheryl had always loved designing and gardening, and she was proficient in bookkeeping and accounting. It was a perfect moonlighting situation. After a while, however, she started to feel torn. She wanted to devote more time to the business she shared with her husband, but she was reluctant to leave Redmond Hair Products. She felt a deep loyalty to Tom Redmond and his company for seeing her through some bad times and for giving her a chance to master the workplace so successfully. Cheryl made her move only when Redmond was unexpectedly bought. She had built her career with one of the best family-friendly businesses an employee could hope for and had learned under the tutelage of a boss who supported women and believed in giving employees flexible time so that they could have a personal and professional life. And with the help of her earnings, she and her husband had renovated the perfect Minnesota farmhouse. Life was good, and now Cheryl needed to take the next step.

In order to jump feet-first into the landscaping business, she needed skills in construction and estimating. Following the lead of her former boss, she enrolled in school, this time on her own dime, at a little technology college that specialized in horticulture and landscaping. There she learned about measurements and scales and more than she ever thought she would know about perennials, trees, and shrubs. She moved her office into her home (from Redmond) and created a filing system for payable vendors as well as estimates and statements on her computer. Now she spends her day as a landscape designer on job sites, conducting estimates and spray-painting designs on the patio for her employees to follow. She uses her experience at Redmond to interact well with her customers and has made them her first priority.

Cheryl flops into bed exhausted, but happy, with "a contentment that comes," she says "from owning my own business." Her message to the rest of us: "It's never too late. Don't look back. Just try. Because if you try and fail, that's much better than living with the regret of not having tried at all. The one thing I don't want in life," she says, "is to be old and to look back and have to say 'What if?'"

# POPULAR MECHANICS

Ren Volpe was fresh out of college with a bachelor's degree in philosophy when she decided to take a cross-country trip in her favorite beat-up car. She had watched as all her friends took office jobs, but she knew that she was not the kind of person who could sit behind a desk for very long. So a trip through the wide open spaces seemed like a good idea.

Before she began her motor adventure, Ren took a course at a training school. She wanted to learn how to fix her car, just in case she found herself in the middle of a Kansas cornfield with a broken-down vehicle. Ren loved the course. She enjoyed the process of learning about her car and the confidence it gave her. She may even have been the only cross-country driver who hoped her vehicle would break down! Ironically, Ren says, her "car didn't break down once." She had the same car for thirteen years, and it often broke down right in front of her house. But never in a cornfield.

By the time Ren got to San Francisco, she needed a job. Since there wasn't a huge demand for philosophers, and since she had enjoyed her brief stint at trade school, she decided to give auto mechanics a whirl. Answering an ad for male and female mechanics, Ren got a job as an apprentice mechanic, quickly building up her skills to the point where she became known as the "lady mechanic."

Ren eventually started her own garage, where ninety percent of her clients were women. She eventually taught auto mechanics to five hundred students and even wrote a book, *The Lady Mechanic's Total Car Care for the Clueless.* After all, she figured, at least half of the people who need their cars

239

fixed are women. Ren figured she was filling a void. Now, at thirty-six, she has gone back to school to get a master's degree in library science. Having had her first child, Ren thinks it is imperative for women who have labored at physical jobs to get skilled in other areas. The body eventually breaks down, and you need to have an alternative way to make a living.

Doing something nontraditional gives you confidence. Nevertheless, even if what you do is different, it may be the only thing that you can do. At some point, it's time to move on. So now Ren is looking forward to taking her library skills into schools to work with children.

HOT TIP: "Once you change your career, you can do anything."—*Ren Volpe*

"For a woman to become a mechanic or do anything that's generally thought of as men's work she has to have chutzpah," says Ren. She didn't start out with a passion for cars. She didn't drive until she was nineteen years old. "I did have the curiosity to always be taking things apart, though. And I had a level of skill with my hands, a lot of manual dexterity and eye coordination, which is important as a mechanic. It's important to understand why you want to enter a nontraditional profession," adds Ren. "There are women I know who became mechanics for political reasons. But it doesn't work that way. Being a feminist isn't enough. You've got to have some skill and natural ability to build your career."

# LISTEN TO YOUR HEART

Sometimes, if you're lucky, a career can be like a long marriage: a glorious road filled with twists and turns, highs and lows—and always something interesting waiting around the bend. Dorre Lin Ray's career has been like that. She's stayed in the same field for over twenty-three years, always reinventing, refashioning and rejuvenating her approach to the art of healing. The lesson we learn from Dorre and others like her who have stayed passionate about the same career is never to throw out the baby with the bath water. Or, put another way, learn to surmount problems and don't let them distract you from doing what you love—even if it means adjusting your focus.

So often when life isn't going well we tend to point the finger at some external aspect of our lives: our relationships, our finances, and sometimes our career. But Dorre points out to all of us how crucial it is to look inside for the answers to our own problems. She celebrates the joy of being able to pursue the same profession over so many years, making it fresh and keeping it interesting every step of the way. It's rare but so gratifying to encounter a woman who has found a large part of the meaning to her spiritual quest through her work.

Dorre was an undergrad in philosophy and psychology at Iowa State University when she chose to become a chiropractor, a profession considered to be unorthodox thirty years ago. Even as a young woman Dorre was intellectually and spiritually motivated to enter a field where, traditionally, doctors prescribed chemicals for ill health and depression—with very poor results. She was also curious as to why people with unresolved emotional issues often manifested physical symptoms. So, in order to explore her love of psychology with her knowledge of the body, she became a Reichian therapist—a therapist who deals with the body as a warehouse for stored emotions. Dorre was in fundamental agreement with the theory that "if your emotions remain unconscious and unexpressed, you will continue to play the same tape—repeatedly—without ever resolving the problem. And because our bodies are the last to know and express, we need to go inside to uncover the key to our own psychological and physical mysteries.

"The thing about bioenergy therapy and chiropractic work that I love," says Dorre "is the innate intelligence of the body that's reflected in its integrity and spirituality. I love getting to and clearing the thoughts, feelings, and patterns stored in the body. I love getting to the root of what's really going on, and asking all the time *What is the inside source of all this pain and dissatisfaction that we carry?* When I started using this new thought system it was awkward. But now I find that after all these years the more I ask, wait, and receive, the more I feel connected with my higher self-wisdom and love. And this new paradigm and methodology remains for me such amazing and powerful stuff."

And yet, at one point, Dorre became unhappy with what she perceived were the limitations of Reichian therapy and chiropractic work. She had built a full practice and a solid reputation as a health practitioner, but was left feeling disappointed and dissatisfied with some of the results. But rather than abandon ship and get out of the healing business altogether, Dorre went on a mission to find other philosophies and healing systems that would help herself and her patients. This was in the days of Esalen and encounter groups, and Dorre tried many forms of psychological and spiritual healing. Finally, she decided to synthesize Neuro Linguistic Programming (NLP) with her other training, and became certified as a SOT/Cranial Chiropractic Doctor. (Neuro Linguistic Programming is a method that determines how people interpret or process information and then act on it.) This, in turn, opened the door to her teaching NLP to chiropractors so that they could incorporate this model into their work. Invited to teach around the world, Dorre found that her business grew by leaps and bounds. This meant hiring additional professionals to her already full staff. "Basically," says Dorre, "my practice grew into a business, with me as the administrator. Where it used to be just me and the patient, suddenly I had a staff of nine people: a trainer, a physical therapist, several chiropractors, acupuncturists, massage therapists, a nutritionist, hypnotherapists, and an exercise specialist. From that point on everything changed for me. I felt confined, stuck with problem solving and unable to travel because I couldn't leave the office so easily. The paper work and billing procedures were complicated and overwhelming. It was becoming impossible to put my patients first and I was miserable."

So, once again, Dorre had to restructure her professional life. She didn't throw away the idea of serving people, but she did look for a new approach that would satisfy her own soul. After years of taking care of so many people—feeding a staff and shouldering so many responsibilities—Dorre knew she was at a point in her life where she needed a big time-out. She had to take time to reflect, to rest, and to synthesize her experiences to give the burnout a chance to pass and for rejuvenation to begin, so she and her husband pulled up stakes entirely and moved to a small town outside of Colorado Springs. "It was so quiet you could hear the Aspen trees sing," Dorre says. "And what they were telling me was to listen to my inner voice, soften and surrender inside."

We realize not everyone has the time to listen to the Aspen trees, but Dorre could and did take five years off to listen to her voice before she knew what she wanted to do next. At that point she was feeling spiritually fulfilled and more passionate than ever about taking the work she had been exploring for over twenty years to the next level. She and her husband had made good new friends, as well as holding on to the old friendships; their lives felt refreshed and clear. Dorre realized she no longer wanted to be involved with people's problems. She wanted to concentrate on what worked. "So many people are focused on what they don't want that they can't get to what they truly desire. That's because most people aren't ready to let go of their problems and clear out past resentments to forgive themselves and other people. They haven't gone through the emptying out stage—the void." The key to this stage is the willingness to be with the *not knowing,* according to Dorre. "I knew and trusted that this next step would show up, and I wanted to create a paradigm where the people whom I treated came ready and willing to let go of the past and move forward. Some people were willing to shift dramatically. Those were the souls who were ripe and ready for the next level of consciousness. And that's what I am doing now. It seems more information and hoping for the best isn't getting us anywhere but more bogged down. So as of now, I've found a rhythm, a creative writing voice that's comfortable for me and that carries my work forward. I have learned to appreciate who is and who isn't ready to let go of their past, and focus on dealing with people who are ready for new purpose, new attitude, and new choices for their future. I believe that we are the creative forces in our own lives."

"What's the advantage of being over forty and in the same career for so long? I have a kind of fullness and wonderful feeling about myself. I feel good about being able to make my passion for healing and my focus on a healthy happy life last so long. And when I review my past, I'm aware that I've tried, explored and experienced most of the things I wanted to do in my life. My husband is talking of travel and slowing down. I find myself renewed with excitement and inspiration, as I have much to explore and learn from life through my work."

## FIRED UP!

"Basically, I'm just a blood-and-guts kind of person," states Esther Stilitz, a twelve-year veteran of the Minnetaka Fire Department in Wisconsin who answered an advertisement at age forty for firefighters in her local paper. Her husband thought she was crazy, but Esther had always dreamed of fighting fires, and she knew it was now or never.

During her yearlong review period, Esther took responder classes, attended drill sessions, and went to meetings with the fifty-nine men and five other women who were being trained at the same time. She kept herself in shape, working out daily to keep herself strong. Her most exhilarating moment occurred when she went to the third floor of a flaming apartment building and, with flames all around and smoke so thick she couldn't see her own hand, helped pull the ceiling down to get rid of the life-threatening hot spots. "What you always worry about," explains Esther, "is that the floor is going to give out underneath you. So you have to keep an eye on each other."

Esther remembers her own mother dragging her out of bed at three in the morning to go see a fire down the street. She figures it's in her blood, which is a likely theory when you consider that Esther's daughter Alison is also a professional firefighter. For a time they worked for the same department, although they had an agreement never to go into a burning house together.

Now retired from firefighting, Esther still uses her training in her present job as a medical assistant. She remembers one day when a patient suffered a seizure. His head hit the floor, causing massive bleeding. Without ruffling a feather, Esther called Code 68 (the emergency number) and continued to hold the man while he violently seizured. His body was flailing out of control, but Esther talked softly to him while she enlisted the help of five people to help hold him down. Everyone else looked on shocked and horrified, but Esther calmly saw the situation through until the ambulance and police got there. She took control. Esther credits her age with making her better able to deal with emergencies. "I'm not so quick to fly off the handle and in a tight situation can be called upon to be level-headed. I handle stress well."

Now that Esther is fifty-three years old, she has a new dream to become a law enforcement officer. She has joined the police reserve and has already completed a year of training. She loves the idea of community service and says, "I don't care how old I am, I'm bound and determined to *do*."

## KEEP ON TRUCKING

"My entry into trucking started as a joke. I was helping my mom move to Florida after Hurricane Andrew hit, when a neighbor of mine [a trucker] happened to just come in from Miami with a loaded car. So I started helping him with his deliveries too. I kidded, 'You know I ought to go to work for you and get paid for all this driving.' He continued the joke by pulling out a CDL manual [the book that explains how to get a truck drivers's license], but you should have seen his face when I took him up on it. 'Well,' I said, 'If life begins at forty, I'm going to have to find out!' And that's how it began. Fate."

"I'm divorced. My kids are grown . . . I'm a grandmother five times over. But I'd always been the type to jump in with both feet and learn from it all. That's what I did with trucking. I love to travel, and I've got friends and family scattered all over the country. So I thought this would be an opportunity to visit the relatives. I was right.

"I borrowed some money from my old boss and went to trucking school for three weeks. And I got a Florida license to drive what they call an FFE, frozen food express, a fully loaded forty-ton tractor trailer. Even with power steering, I gotta tell you, it's hard to drive. But now I'm used to it. You know, somebody made a comment to me the other day, a man as a matter of fact. He asked, 'How can you do that?' And I looked at him and said, 'You see your little pickup? You get in there and you drive it all over like there's no tomorrow, right?' He goes, 'Yeah.' I said, 'I do the same thing with my truck. I can't drive your pickup. But I can sure drive this thing.'

"I learned determination from my mother. In my formative years she was sick with a disease called scleroderma. At the time they didn't know what it was. She was one of the four diagnosed cases in the country. There were times when my mother should have died, and my dad would look at her and say, 'You really want me to raise these two kids?' And she would fight all over again. Right on her deathbed, and she'd fight back.

"I learned from her that you set your mind to do something, and come hell or high water, you are just flat gonna do it. What's the worst thing anybody is ever going to tell me? No? So fight back. I was trying to get rid of the first truck I bought. It was a lemon and the salesman who had sold it to me told me I couldn't trade it because I had no equity. And he told me to go away. 'You're bothering me. I don't want to hear it. Get out of my face.' So, I'm in a dealership in El Paso and they had a truck I decided I wanted for Christmas. It was the first of August. We went back and forth, but I didn't pursue it. Then my truck went down again. And I called the dealership in Texas, faxed them a credit application. Three hours later he calls me and says, 'When do you want to come and get your truck?' And I walked right back to the original dealership and parked his truck right underneath his nose, and I told him I had bought a second truck where I could get some service.

"I feel the people in my industry respect me. I was featured in *Women in Trucking*. There's more than the skill of driving. You have to know the weather. You watch the clouds. You watch the treetops to see how much wind there is and what direction it's coming from. You get storms that come up suddenly. If you see them coming down the road and you're driving seventy miles per hour and you see a twister, you've gotta get out of it.

"I've always been attracted to all male professions. Maybe because I was a tomboy when I was a girl. I'm still the only girl in a family of cousins and everything. But ironically, being a mother was the best reason for being a trucker. You're up all hours of the day and night with colic or whatever. You put in some very long days as a mom.

"My biggest piece of advice to women who want to do something new is, 'Never Give Up. Don't let them drag you down.' There's a T-shirt running around and it says, 'Mental Anguish. Mental Deficiency. You notice all problems start with MEN.' I agree with that because the men of the world decided that this was their domain and I wasn't getting in. Well, here I am."

# FROM BANKING TO . . .

Sage Vivant was a bank manager who dreamed of becoming a writer. Her biggest complaint was that she felt completely squelched. "It wasn't politically correct to be who I was. I

249

had to be sort of an automaton. Poker-faced. Humor was not highly valued at the bank, nor was any form of creativity. I had some good ideas, and I was tired of having someone telling me why my ideas would fail. I wanted to make my own mistakes and take responsibility."

She left with a package deal that gave her five months out of the rat race to pursue her goal. "I knew that I wanted to write and that I wanted time to be on my own, so I started to think about what people like to read. I knew they liked to read about themselves, and I knew that they liked to read about sex, so I thought if I wrote about them having sex, well, that's a double whammy!

"I've always been a little bit frustrated by the quality of erotica. You buy it to read a good story and to be stimulated, but it can be frustrating. You can waste a lot of time. I'd written some for my own tastes, and I had the feeling that other people would want the same thing. So I devised a brief questionnaire to determine a client's wants. I've been working at this for sixteen months, and it's helping me to reach my goals of running a business, doing good for others, and making me autonomous. Making the move for me wasn't scary. I don't do *scared*. When an idea hits me and a big change confronts me, it's a question of how can I do this really creatively? How can I beat the odds? My passion has always been to feel like I'm contributing to the world. I'm not quite there yet, but I am making couples happy. I'm making individuals happy. I'm allowing people to explore some sexual facets of themselves that they might not be able to do without fiction and fantasy.

"I'm actually amazed at how accepting my parents have been. And encouraging. My mother said, 'Well, I'd rather you were writing bedtime stories for children than for adults.' But I think they're struck by the inventiveness of the whole product and service. When I first started, I had no idea how to price my stories. Now I charge two hundred and twenty-five dollars a story, and I think that's about where it's going to stay.

"I market myself by doing interviews, TV and radio, and press releases in different parts of the country. My advice to someone wanting to go out on her own? Let the world know who you are. If you're doing something even remotely interesting, tell the world about it. Blanket radio stations. Blanket newspapers. I even took a half-day class at Media Alliance to learn how to do a press release and how to get my word out to the media. When I saw how easy it was to write a press release, I started to blitz the world. With the advent of computers, God, you don't even need a fax machine. Your fax is on the computer. You do it. You send it out. That's it.

"The future? I was reading an interview with a famous rock and roller who's now in his fifties, and he said, 'I really don't know what it is that I want to do yet. I think that when you figure it out, you're kind of all done.' And I thought, *that's absolutely right.* So I cut it out and put it on my computer.

"For years I used to kick myself when someone would ask me in a job interview, 'Where do you want to be in five or ten years?' I never had an answer, and I thought this must mean that I have no direction in life; that I'm such a loser. I've got to get a goal because I don't know where I want to be in ten years. Now I want to see what happens. It keeps me open and flexible so I don't miss any opportunities."

# Chapter Ten

# If I Don't
# Do It Now

Age does not define us. Attitude does. If you feel dissatisfied, burned out, given the shaft, or just plain bored, then get thee to a nunnery, a spa, a therapist, a best friend, a cruise, or a swing dance class. Anything that's going to give you a fresh start and a new perspective. Think of yourself as a great American novel. The middle may seem slow and tedious, a bit of an effort to get through . . . but then the passion picks up, the plot develops, and the characters deepen. Now you read slowly, hoping it will never end. Remind you of anything?

If you take only one piece of advice from this book make it this: Live as if your best years are in front of you, not behind you. All the practical tools for a career transition can be wound around this philosophy. And must. All we can hope to do is provide you with a kick in the panty hose to remind you that you are responsible for your life and the direction it takes. Go see a prospective employer and present him or her with your transferable skills and an energetic résumé, and doors will open. Go in armed with a great attitude, a sense of humor, and an excitement about the world around you . . . well, we can't guarantee that you won't be held hostage until you agree to sign your employment contract right there. It's simple. People hire people they want to be around. People with a twinkle in their eye and a hand in the cookie jar. People with a wise and generous nature who have something to offer that goes beyond the job description.

Stop thinking that just because you're older you have the god-given right to kvetch about everything and everyone. Lose the conversation about the tendinitis in your arm and any sentence that starts with "In my day" or "At my age." Otherwise you'll be relegated to the backroom mah jong game. By the same token, don't talk up some accomplishment of twenty years ago. Nobody wants to hear about Woodstock, your early sixties foray into communal living, or almost meeting Gloria Steinem. Better to recall your accomplishments of the last twelve months when you organized a successful fund-raiser for your favorite charity, came up with an idea that helped revolutionize or at least modify your workplace, wrote an editorial for your local newspaper, found three helpful time-saving sites on the web, and invested in a stock that nobody else believed in but just went through the roof. That's progress. And that's what people want to hear.

Have you noticed that as we get older we automatically say no to trying anything new? We fall back on the house special, friends we've known forever, even ways of interacting with our partners or children. We become such creatures of habit and comfort. We're not suggesting you jump out of an airplane to celebrate your birthday, but before you automatically say no to anything new, take a beat. Try saying yes.

It's important to keep career change in perspective. We all have a friend or two whose lives have been challenging—illness, problems with children, divorce. . . . These are the issues that require courage and stamina. You know that. Keep a perspective on your goal. Be happy for what you have and approach your career change with that attitude. We want you to achieve the career of your dreams too. But before you embark on this process, take a moment to appreciate all you have been given and all you have created for yourself.

Do something that satisfies your soul—as a source of pride or satisfaction and as a way of giving back, leaving a legacy for the generations to come.

Take a look in the mirror. The little wrinkles around your eyes may testify to your wisdom, but that's no reason you can't treat yourself to a spiffy new haircut with a stylist you've seen in a magazine. We're at a point in our lives where we don't lead with our looks, where we're no longer the babe. So what. Attractiveness can be achieved without cleavage and bare midriffs. We can also be a little thankful and somewhat smug that we missed the dark brown lipstick and piercing fads. On the other hand, we were in time for the lasers and collagen that saved some of us from going under the knife . . . not to mention those self-tanners that kept our skin smooth. Our looks no longer get in the way. Now someone who wants us wants the whole package—and what a package that is. Make yourself over to the point where three people stop you and tell you look great. Better yet, make yourself over to the point where you believe them.

Don't forget to pray. To laugh. To meditate. Write a letter to someone you've been out of contact with for years. Clean up old resentments and miscommunications. Dump all that toxic stuff out of your life and begin relationships anew. Read a great book from cover to cover till three in the morning. Try green tea. Really learn what a database means. And then tell us. Buy fresh flowers, just because. Take an art class. Walk on a beach. Buy three new CDs by artists you've never sampled. Try one new lipstick. Now kiss someone. And from the perspective of this new outlook, refreshed and raring to go, look back at your makeover and start all over again. The process of change and renewal never ends. Besides, what do you have to lose? Because as two old wise girls once said, "If you don't do it now? . . ." well, you know.

# And now
# a word from
# our authors . . .

It was 1968 (and what began 33 years ago as just a job and a way for a single mother to pay her bills has grown into a gratifying and successful career. It's challenging to help great companies find talented people and talented people find satisfying careers, and ultimately it's very rewarding.

For me, the art of interviewing people, helping candidates find their strengths, and placing them with companies seems as familiar as brushing my teeth. Yet I know that throughout the years I have been able to keep my business exciting and stimulating by constantly following business trends and adapting to the ever-changing workplace. Executive search is a complex business that combines the skill sets of a private detective, a psychologist, a masterful salesperson, and a shrewd negotiator. That is the background that has allowed me to turn out a book based on real experience, with real people and real case studies.

Writing this book has given me the opportunity to share my knowledge and experience with you. I hope that you will find inspiration and your own path to success.

*Pamela*

My inspiration to write this book came from attending too many cocktail parties where people always wanted to know how I managed to enjoy several professional incarnations, all of them exciting and seemingly random. I began my work life as a psychologist and quickly realized it was not the high-octane job my natural metabolism required. So I transferred my active listening skills and writing ability to television, working as a talk show host, and eventually ending up as an LA correspondent for the CBS Evening News with Dan Rather. My next step was to leave journalism and pursue Hollywood where, through imagination, chutzpah, and an enlightened mentor by the name of Michael Douglas, I became Vice President of Production for his newly formed Stonebridge Entertainment. Today I continue to write and produce under my own banner of NayNay Films, and speak to groups across the country not only about the process of re-invention, but the problem all corporations face today—employee retention.

I had always thought that luck was a factor in my working life (you know, being in the right place at the right time), but at a certain point I had to admit that my talent for changing careers was not connected with the zodiac. I have been able to segue from one career to another because I have been able to transfer the skills I had accumulated in one career and apply them to the next. I firmly believe that any woman can take anything she's learned personally and professionally and apply those lessons to her dream career. And if you see me at a cocktail party, please don't hesitate to ask me how you can realize your dream too. After all, If You Don't Do It Now . . . well, you know.

*Nadine Schiff*

# Resource Guide

We've done our best to give you the tools to go about conducting your career makeover. That's not to say, though, that you won't want to turn somewhere else for guidance. You need more than one girlfriend to get through life, and you may need more than one book to get you on your way. We understand. (It's not like that time you went to see *The English Patient* with one friend after you promised you'd go with another. . . .) In any case, these are just some of the many resources available to you. We're listing them here to help you get started. We're not recommending any of these books or web sites. We merely want to point you in the right direction. As we've said before, the rest is up to you.

# BOOKS

## Business Management

**The A-To-Z Book of Managing People,** by Victoria Kaplan, Robert Kunreuther (contributor). Berkley Pub Group, 1996
 A good resource for anyone who has to manage people. Especially useful for new managers.

## Corporate Culture

**The New Corporate Cultures: Revitalizing the Workplace after Downsizing, Mergers, and Reengineering,** by Terrence E. Deal, Allan A. Kennedy. Perseus Press, 1999
 An intelligent book that recognizes the importance of corporate culture and details the changes—mostly negative—that dominate workplace culture.

**The Corporate Culture Survival Guide,** by Edgar H. Schein (preface), Warren G. Bennis. Jossey-Bass, 1999
 Why we all need to care about corporate culture.

## Home-Based Businesses

**101 Best Home-Based Businesses for Women, Revised 2nd Edition,** by Priscilla Y. Huff. Prime Publishing, 1998
 Solid advice on what to consider when launching your home-based business. Includes plenty of *been-there, done-that* stories.

**The Best Home Businesses for the 21st Century: The Inside Information You Need to Know to Select a Home-Based Business That's Right for You,** by Paul Edwards, Sarah Edwards, Tarcher, 1999

The third edition of this compendium explores the advantages and disadvantages of home-based businesses, while providing comprehensive profiles of more than one hundred hot new business opportunities for self-employment.

(And don't forget to check out your local or on-line bookseller for books directly related to your product or service. You can find books on how to start a home-based business on just about everything, from gift baskets to landscaping to catering and antiques.)

## The Internet

**The Soul of the New Consumer: The Attitudes, Behavior, and Preferences of E-Customers,** by Laurie Windham, Ken Orton (contributor). Allworth Press, 2000

Look here for the lowdown on the behavior of Internet consumers.

**101 Ways to Promote Your Web Site: Filled With Proven Internet Marketing Tips, Tools, Techniques, and Resources to Increase Your Web Site Traffic,** by Susan Sweeney. Maximum Press, 2000

In addition to providing guidance on how to launch a web site, make use of off-line promotion and marketing in news groups, this book of wizardry includes information on such things as search engines, signature files, link trading, traffic analysis, webcasting—and other things we don't understand.

**eBrands: Building an Internet Business at Breakneck Speed,** by Phil Carpenter. Harvard Business School Press, 2000
A good primer on how to stand out in an environment characterized by choice.

## Job Hunting

**Electronic Resumes & Online Networking: How to Use the Internet to Do a Better Job Search, Including a Complete, Up-To-Date Resource Guide,** by Rebecca Smith. Career Press, 1999
Innovative ways of conducting your on-line job search. Chock-full of strategies and resources.

**Job Searching Online For Dummies®,** by Pam Dixon. IDG Books Worldwide, 1998
Great ideas for jump-starting your search.

**The Complete Q&A Job Interview Book, 2nd Edition,** by Jeffrey G. Allen. John Wiley & Sons, 1997
A bestseller that includes practice scripts and interview questions.

## Marketing

**EVEolution: The Eight Truths of Marketing to Women,** by Faith Popcorn, Lys Marigold. Hyperion, 2000
A sensible and intelligent book about marketing to women. Finally.

**The One-Day Marketing Plan: Organizing and Completing a Plan That Works** by Roman G. Hiebing, Jr.; Scott W. Cooper. NTC Publishing, 1999

This new edition of the best-selling guide provides the reader with ten basic steps to market any product or service.

**1,001 Ways to Keep Customers Coming Back,** by Donna Greiner, Theodore B. Kinni, Seth Godin. Prima Publishing, 1999

Eleven broad strategies on keeping your customers happy.

## *Networking*

**Creating Women's Networks: A How-To Guide for Women and Companies (Jossey-Bass Business & Management Series)** by Catalyst, et al. Jossey-Bass, 1998

A comprehensive manual for getting ahead by getting together, from Catalyst, a not-for-profit group dedicated to helping women achieve their full professional potential.

## *Sales and Negotiating*

**Close the Deal: 120 Checklists to Help You Close the Very Best Deal** by Sam Deep, Lyle Sussman. Perseus Press, 1999

Clear, practical advice on how to sharpen your sales skills based on programs developed at the Sandler Sales Institute.

**The Greatest Salesman in the World,** by Og Mandino. Bantam Books, 1983

First published in 1968 and still going strong. What more can we say?

**The Shadow Negotiation: How Women Can Master the Hidden Agendas That Determine Bargaining Success,** by Deborah M. Kolb, Judith Williams. Simon & Schuster, 2000.

This book talks about the unspoken attitudes and hidden assumptions that often govern the negotiating process. And it's written by women!

**Getting to Yes: Negotiating Agreement Without Giving In** by Roger Fisher, William Ury, Bruce Patton (Editor). Penguin, 1992

The classic text on negotiation. Worth a look.

**You Can Negotiate Anything,** by Herb Cohen. Bantam Books, 1989

Another popular classic. This one's been in print for over twenty years.

*Starting Your Own Business*

**Start Your Own Business: The Only Start-Up Book You'll Ever Need,** by Rieva Lesonsky, (Editor). Entrepreneur Media Inc., 1998

Put together by Rieva Lesonsky and the staff of *Entrepreneur* magazine, this comprehensive guide covers the basics and then some.

**Small Business For Dummies®,** by Eric Tyson, Jim Schell. IDG Books, 1998

A common-sense advice book on how to get started that actually explains the difference between a company and a corporation. (And no, we don't like the title either.)

**Glorious Accidents: How Everyday Americans Create Thriving Companies,** by Michael J. Glauser. Shadow Mountain, 1998

Lots of *been there, done that* advice in this book. Worth a look even if you aren't thinking of starting your own business.

**Anatomy of a Business Plan: A Step-by-Step Guide to Starting Smart, Building the Business, and Securing Your Company's Future (Anatomy of a Business),** by Linda Pinson, Jerry Jinnett. Dearborn Trade, 1999

The fourth edition of this popular book will show you how to create a professional business plan. Simple and easy to follow.

# WEB SITES

We could write a book on web sites useful to women who want to undergo career makeovers—maybe we will! In the meantime, though, you may find it helpful to check out our sample sites listed below. You never know where your clicking will take you.

- http://www.sba.gov

The web site of the Small Business Administration provides a wealth of information and assistance, from financing your small business through its loan program to complying with government tax mandates.

- http://www.digital-women.com/

This fun site bills itself as an "international community for women in business." A comprehensive address that's well worth a visit, it offers a great list of *how to's*—from how to design a business card, to how to set up a budget—and a nifty roundtable providing women with a forum in which to barter their products and services.

- http://herassistant.com

A great web site with interesting daily clicks, a pretty exhaustive archive of articles, and an interactive forum geared specifically towards women and their businesses.

- http://momsnetwork.com

momsnetwork gives work-at-home moms the resources they need to balance their lives and promote their businesses. You'll find some pretty clever tips here.

- http://nafe.com

Women's associations abound on the web. Check out this site, which belongs to The National Associate for Female Executive. It's a good place to start.

- http://www2.homefair.com

This site includes one of the best little gadgets we've seen on-line! Want to move to New York City from, say, Huntsville, Alabama? Then log on here and try the salary calculator to see what you'd have to earn to sustain the same standard of living. (Oh . . . if you're interested, $50,000 in Huntsville is the equivalent of $116,344 in New York City. Thought you'd like to know.)

- **http://www.dol.gov**

Log on to the Department of Labor's web site for programs, services, and—perhaps most important to anyone starting her own business—laws and regulations. Go to

> http://www.dol.gov/dol/asp/public/programs/
> handbook/contents.htm

to learn about the laws, regulations and technical assistance services appropriate to small businesses.

Check out these great places to enhance your search:

jobs.com, monster.com, jobsonline.com, headhunters.com, futuresetp.com, jobboards.com, career.com, advancingwomen.com, womerica.com, allforwomen.com, sitesforwomen.com, pioneerthinking.com, freeality.com, careerwomen.com, careerbabe.com, top100womensites.com, careerbuilder.com, careermosaic.com, and careerpath.com.

**And, whatever you do,
don't forget to check out our web site:
ifidontdoitnow.com**

# Acknowledgments

For our partners-in-crime—Michael Schiff and Robert Hollander—*If I Don't Do It Now* . . . meant you had to wait. We love you and thank you for your patience.

For our parents: Dena and Max and Dulcy and Marty.

To our agent extraordinaire, the great Jan Miller who worked with us from the conception of the idea to the birth of the book. . . . We are grateful for your support, friendship, and dinners at the Bel Air Hotel. We love your guts. And to her assistant Shannon who worked tirelessly for us every step of the way.

Thanks to our new friends at Simon & Schuster: Judith Curr, Karen Mender, Tracy Behar, Brenda Copeland, Laurie Commaccio, Melinda Mullin, Laura Mullen, and Robin Kessler. We don't know how you do what you do . . . but please don't change careers until after the one hundredth printing.

Many thanks to Elizabeth Faraut for a research job well done . . . through two pregnancies. You are amazing.

Kudos to Joanne Mills and Shirley Hughley for office support. And a special thank you to Melissa Feeley. By the time this book hits the shelves we hope you're well on your way to your new career as an MTV diva. Our thanks to Steven Spector for sharing cramped office space without complaint. Warm thanks to Michale Canale for opening his salon for the makeovers.

For our friend Annie Gilbar who lovingly sat with us for many hours . . . with her red pen, Post-its, and iced tea.

And to Maria Shriver, great girlfriend and author in her own right . . . who put her own books aside to champion ours. You are a blessing in our lives.

To our gang who showed us constant support and inspiration: David Brody, Susan Hasazi, Carole Isenberg, Rhea Perlman, Jack Steinfeld, Cristina Ferrare, and Kelly Chapman Meyer. We now have time for lunch.

To Johanna and Joel and Lindsay and Matthew. You continue to enrich our lives.

And to all the women who shared their stories with us so willingly in order to help other women find their voice . . . and a new career. . . . March right to the big corner office and collect your good karma. You deserve the best for wanting the best not just for yourselves—but for all of us.

*Nadine and Pamela*

# Index

African-Americans, 163–65,
    227–30
analytical skills, 24
assets, evaluating, 54–55
attitude, 20–23, 127
    if you don't do it now, 252–
    55
attractiveness, 126, 254

bastards, 51–52
business plans, 204–05

capital and entrepreneurship,
    205–06
career makeover basics, 94–
    137
    cover letters, 115–16
    follow through, 135–37
    interviews, *see* interviews
    résumés, *see* résumés
career makeovers:
    asking hard questions, 12,
    13

basics of, *see* career makeover
    basics
examples of, 15–16, 73–88,
    128–33
as getting easier as you get older,
    13–14
midlife women and, 11–15
need for, 10–16
signs indicating need for, 11–12
changing your career, 53–93
    career-emergency marketing
    plan, *see* marketing plan,
    career-emergency
    career makeover examples,
    73–88
    defining your passion, 53–55
    evaluating your assets, 54–55
    getting unstuck, 71–73
    if you don't do it now, 252–55
    know-thyself guide to, 55–59
    as others view you, 59–60
    unzip yourself test, 61–71
child care, 207

chivalry, 51
chronological résumés, 96–97
    example of, 107–10
classes, 73
cold-calling, 92
committee interviews, 120–22
common ground, 43
corporate culture, 138–66
    books on, 262
    changing, 156
    checklist to assess, 157–59
    determining, prior to
        employment, 156–57
    determining the type you want,
        149
    first impression of, 139, 147,
        159–60
    interviews and, 159
    research on, 138–39
    sexual and hierarchical politics,
        150–51
    size of company and, 152–56
    stories that illustrate, 139–56,
        160–66
    top down, 153–54
    values and, 151–52
corporate web sites, 30–31
cover letters, 115–16
creative skills, 25

dinner or lunch interview, 119–20
direct marketing, 188–89
dream jobs, 221–51
    banking to . . . , 249–51
    Broadway to Bali, 230–33
    fired up, 245–47
    flight attendant to bed and
        breakfast proprietor, 227–30
    generally, 221–22
    hair care to horticulture, 235–38

    keep on trucking, 247–49
    listen to your heart, 241–45
    player to performer, 233–35
    popular mechanics, 239–40
    product manager to film buff,
        222–27

enterprise, becoming your own,
    89–90
entrepreneurship, 200–20
    books on, 266–67
    capital, 205–06
    designing a business plan,
        204–05
    doing what you know, 203–04
    generally, 200–01
    home-based, *see* home-based
        businesses
    marketing yourself, 206
    personal happiness and, 201–02
    professional and personal goals
        and, 202–03
    working from home, *see*
        working from home
executive recruiters, 91–92

follow up, 93
functional résumés, 97–99
    example of, 111–14

goals, entrepreneurship and,
    202–03
grace under fire, 51–52, 126–27

home-based businesses, 207–20
    books on, 262–63
    child care, 207
    contact, 208
    office hours, 207–08
    pj alert, 208

relax, 209
scalable facilities, 209–10
space, 207
stories that illustrate, 209–14
technology, 209
working from home, *see*
  working from home
human relationships, *see*
  networking

if I don't do it now, 252–55
information interviews, 118–19
intangible sales, 169
interests, listing, 72
Internet, 178–99
  baby-boomers and, 196
  be who you are, 191–93
  books on, 263–64
  corporate web sites, 30–31
  direct marketing and, 188–89
  dot-com companies, 156
  editorial backgrounds and, 189
  intimidation by, 189–90
  job search and, 31, 182–83
  key positions in companies, 188
  lack of experience and, 192
  marketing experience and, 197
  networking and, 37, 183–84,
    195
  passion for, 190–91
  personal advantages, 193–94
  researching the new technology,
    191
  sales careers and, 176–77,
    194–95, 198
  as something new, 195
  start-ups, 180–82
  staying current and, 36–37
  success stories, 178–87, 191–92,
    198–99

women and, 179, 196
interviewers, 133–35
  distracted, 135
  hostile, 134
  interview process and, 122
  off topic, 134–35
  rapport with, 117, 122, 125–26
  yakkers, 133–34
  youth of, 116
interviews, 116–37
  attitude and, 20–22, 127
  career turn-ons and, 123, 124
  clothing for, 118
  committee, 120–22
  corporate culture and, 159
  corporate web sites and, 30–31
  dinner or lunch, 119–20
  enthusiasm and, 123–24
  following up on, 135–37
  generally, 117–18, 121
  grace under pressure and, 126–27
  information, 118–19
  interest in the process, 123
  from interviewer's point of view,
    122
  long view and, 124
  optimism and, 123, 124
  physical makeover and, 126
  preparation for, 121, 125
  questions asked during, 119
  research and, 30–32
  skills and, 28
  taking control of, 125
  teamwork and, 127
  for those over thirty-five, 122–27
  tooting your own horn, 121,
    125, 127
  transferable skills and, 126
  youthful qualities, 123–24
  *see also* interviewers

job search, 31, 182–83
  books on, 264

karma, 127
know-thyself guide, 55–59

leap of faith, 23
"left-brained" skills, 24
leveraging your skills, *see* skills
likeability, 20–21, 34, 117, 253
"loves" and "hates," 53–54, 72
loyalty, 14–15

manual dexterity, 25
marketing:
  books on, 264–65
  experience in, 197
marketing plan, career-emergency,
    88–93
  become your own enterprise,
    89–90
  cold-call, 92
  executive recruiters, 91–92
  follow up, 93
  proactivity, 89
  record-keeping, 93
  target your résumés, 91
marketing yourself, 206
mentors, 44–48
  acquiring, 44–45
  beyond the workplace, 47–48
  corporate culture and, 162,
    164–65
  entrepreneurship and, 202
  negative experiences and, 45–47
  trends and, 46
mind your own business, *see*
    entrepreneurship
moonlighters, *see w*orking from
    home

networking:
  book on, 265
  entrepreneurship and, 206
  former co-workers and, 41–42
  Internet and, 37, 183–84, 195
  mentors and, 45
  sales careers and, 168
  as seventh Commandment,
    40–43
  virtual corporations and, 29–30
  working from home and, 219
  as you get older, 42–43
  with younger colleagues, 43

others' view of you, 59–60
  sample questions, 60

packaging yourself, 29
passions, defining your, 53–55
  Internet and, 190–91
people skills, 24–25
perseverance, 136–37
physical makeover, 126, 254
proactivity, 88
promoting yourself, 32–34

reading, 73
record-keeping, 93
research:
  on companies that interest you,
    72–73
  corporate culture and, 138–39
  interviews and, 30–32, 121, 125
  trends and, 39
  virtual corporations and, 30–32
resource guide, 262–69
  books, 262–67
  web sites, 267–69
résumés, 94–114
  attitude and, 95

chronological, 96–97, 107–10
    focus and, 96
    functional, 97–99, 111–14
    generally, 94–95
    targeting, 91
    updating, 96
    writing tips, 99–106
"right-brained" skills, 25

sales careers, 167–77
    books on, 265–66
    gender and, 168–69
    intangible sales, 169
    Internet, 176–77, 194–95, 198
    networking and, 168
    requirements for, 168
    skills from personal life and,
        174–76
    stories that illustrate, 170–77
    tangible sales, 169
saying Yes!, 34, 253–54
self-confidence, 20–23
self-knowledge:
    defining your passions, 53–54
    evaluating your assets, 54–55
    know-thyself guide to, 55–59
    as others view you, 59–60
    unzip yourself test, 61–71
self-promotion, 32–34
sense of humor, 34, 117, 253
sexual politics, 150–51
showing off your skills, 34–36
skills, 23–28
    analytical, 24
    articulating, 27–28
    creative, 25
    listing your own, 25–26, 72
    manual dexterity, 25
    people, 24–25
    showing off your, 34–36

socializing off-site, 151
starting your own business, *see*
    entrepreneurship
staying current, 36–40

tangible assets, 169
telecommuters, *see* working from
    home
tenacity, 39
Ten Commandments, 17–52
    become your own virtual
        corporation, 28–32
    don't let the bastards get you
        down, 51–52
    get attitude, 20–23
    leverage your own skills, 23–28
    mentors, 44–48
    networking, 40–43
    promote yourself, 32–34
    show off your skills, 34–36
    tap into trends, 36–40
    volunteerism, 48–50
trends, 36–40
    mentors and, 46

unsticking yourself, 71–73
unzipping yourself, *see* changing
    your career

validating relationships, 23
values, corporate culture and, 151
virtual corporation, 28–32
    defined, 28–29
    networking and, 29–30
    research and, 30–32
virtual staffers, *see* working from
    home
volunteerism:
    entrepreneurship and, 201–02
    getting unstuck and, 73

volunteerism (*continued*)
  new careers and, 49–50
  as the ninth Commandment,
    48–50
  at work, 34–35

web sites:
  corporate, 30–31
  resource guide, 267–69
working from home, 214–20
  advantages of, 214–15

boundaries and, 215–16
difficulties with, 218
increasing popularity of, 216
names for, 214
office politics and, 218
preparation for, 216–17
raising children and, 215,
  218
stories that illustrate, 217–20
teamwork and, 217
World Wide Web, 198

Printed in the United States
by Baker & Taylor Publisher Services